Easy
Cricut® Crafts

Easy SVG Downloads!

Download all the ready-to-use SVG files for the projects in this book at the following link:

www.betterdaybooks.com/easy-cricut-crafts-svg-download

Easy Cricut® Crafts © 2022 by Cori George and Better Day Books, Inc.

This book is a revised edition of *Cut & Craft*, published by Leisure Arts, Inc., 104 Champs Blvd., STE 100, Maumelle, AR 72113-6738.

Leisure Arts has been inspiring the creative community since 1971 with innovative craft products, books, and more! For more info, please visit *www.leisurearts.com*.

Publisher: Peg Couch
Cover/Book Designer: Lori Malkin Ehrlich
Graphic Artist (*Cut & Craft*): Beth Oberholtzer
Editor: Colleen Dorsey
Technical Editor (*Cut & Craft*): Denise Russell
Photostylist: Lori Wenger
Photographer: Jason Masters

Library of Congress Control Number: 2022940611
ISBN: 978-0-7643-6548-5
Printed in China
First printing
Copublished by Better Day Books, Inc., and Schiffer Publishing, Ltd.

BETTER DAY BOOKS®

Better Day Books
P.O. Box 21462
York, PA 17402
Phone: 717-487-5523
Email: hello@betterdaybooks.com
www.betterdaybooks.com
 @better_day_books

SCHIFFER PUBLISHING

Schiffer Publishing
4880 Lower Valley Road
Atglen, PA 19310
Phone: 610-593-1777
Fax: 610-593-2002
Email: info@schifferbooks.com
www.schifferbooks.com

This title is available for promotional or commercial use, including special editions. Contact info@schifferbooks.com for more information.

Easy Cricut® Crafts

More Than 35 Quick, Easy, and Stylish Cutting Machine Projects Using Vinyl, Iron-On, Cardstock, Cork, Leather, and Fabric

Cori George

BETTER DAY BOOKS®

HAPPY · CREATIVE · CURATED

Contents

14

26

32

42

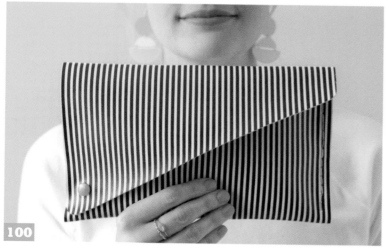

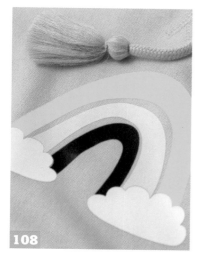

122

126

134

136

140

152

160

170

166

DREAM BIG

184

180

Letter from the Author

Hello!

When I first learned about electronic cutting machines, I thought they were primarily for scrapbookers—embellish a scrapbook spread with cutouts, cut some cute cardstock letters, and that's about it. But when I got one into my studio and started playing around, I was amazed by all of the different projects I could make. From home décor to apparel, organization solutions to party supplies—there was so much I was able to create using my cutting machine! I put down my scissors and never looked back.

Over the past few years, I've become comfortable using my cutting machine with an array of different materials. I've cut gorgeous felt flowers, wood home décor projects, and more paper party decorations than I can count. I've cut adhesive vinyl labels to organize everything in our home. I've made leather jewelry, vacation T-shirts, and cork coasters. I've even cut fabric pieces to make several quilts! This book will take you outside your comfort zone and get you as excited about all of these materials as I am.

Each cutting machine is different, so you will need to consult the user guide to get instructions for cutting individual materials on your machine. Each machine comes with different blades, mats, and tools—it's far too extensive to cover in a single book. My goal in this book is not to help you learn how to use your specific machine; instead, I want to inspire you to cut a wide assortment of materials and use them on blank base materials you may never have thought to use. You're going to make so much more with your cutting machine!

Yours creatively,

Cori

About the Author

Cori George is the creative mind behind the website and digital shop Hey, Let's Make Stuff. Based in Washington State, she loves inspiring half a million women every month to make their lives more fun with easy cutting machine crafts, digital downloads, and simple DIY tutorials. When she's not crafting, she loves traveling, strong coffee, and spending quality time with her husband and adorable twin boys. Her first book, *Paper Party*, was released by Leisure Arts in 2018. You can learn more about Cori at *www.heyletsmakestuff.com*. If you have any questions about the SVG files in this book, please email help@heyletsmakestuff.com.

Getting Started

New to electronic cutting machines? Don't worry—once you learn the basics covered in the next few pages, you'll be ready to rock and roll and start creating your own awesome projects. These pages are also a handy reference as you make the items in this book, so bookmark them now!

Cutting Machines

Choosing a cutting machine can be a big (and expensive!) decision. Your choice will depend on features, price, and the types of crafts you want to make with it. Here are some of the top machines on the market today and an overview of their capabilities.

Cricut Maker® Series

Cricut Maker series machines are Cricut's top-of-the-line machines. Along with all the standard cutting-machine materials like paper, adhesive vinyl, and iron-on vinyl, Cricut Maker can cut materials up to 2mm thick using its knife blade—including wood, leather, chipboard, and more. It also has a rotary blade for cutting fabric, felt, and other "shifty" materials.

In addition to cutting, Cricut Maker can also write, score, engrave, deboss, and perforate, using additional tools. The Adaptive Tool System on Cricut Maker allows Cricut to add more tools and capabilities in the future.

Cricut mats come in both 12" x 12" and 12" x 24" in a variety of "grips." All Cricut machines use the Cricut Design Space® software. You can upload to the software the free SVG files in this book and begin cutting. Cricut Maker is the machine I used to create the projects in this book.

Cricut Explore® Series

Cricut Explore series machines are a great option for most crafters, especially those who don't want to spend the extra money on the upgraded cutting capabilities of Cricut Maker. Cricut Explore machines have precise cutting, scoring, and writing capabilities so you can make a wide variety of projects with most of the materials in this book. Cricut Explore is a great all-around machine—I have one in addition to my Cricut Maker and use it all the time in my studio.

Cricut Joy™

Cricut Joy is Cricut's smallest cutting machine, with a cut width of only 4½". This machine is great for making smaller, simpler projects like cards and vinyl decals. Because of the limited cutting size and fewer machine tools, many of the projects in this book cannot be made using Cricut Joy.

Other Machines

Silhouette Cameo® 4

The Silhouette Cameo 4 is Silhouette's newest machine. Some of the unique features of this machine include a built-in feed roller so you can easily cut 10' of a continuous adhesive vinyl and iron-on vinyl without a mat, a 3mm clearance for thicker materials using its kraft blade, and a rotary cutter for fabric. It also cuts up to 12" in width and comes in a 15" Plus version as well.

Silhouette mats come in both 12" x 12" and 12" x 24" in a variety of "tacks." Many users find the Silhouette Studio® software to be easy to use. To use the SVG files in this book, you will need to upgrade to the Silhouette Studio® Designer Edition software.

Brother ScanNCut DX

The Brother ScanNCut DX, which has a loyal following, has a built-in scanner, detects materials automatically, and includes hundreds of designs and a handful of fonts. Like the Silhouette, it has mat-free feeding, which means you can cut adhesive vinyl and iron-on vinyl up to 6' long.

Brother mats come only in 12" x 12" in a variety of "tacks." Though the ScanNCut works as a stand-alone machine without a computer, you will need to connect it to a device to upload the SVG files in this book.

Purchasing your first electronic cutting machine is a very personal decision. Find the brand and machine that works for you, and work with what you have—if your machine doesn't have the exact functionality listed in a specific project, you can often adapt by using different materials, sizes, or even techniques. And follow your machine's manufacturer on social media to learn about future innovations and releases for your machine!

Blades, Mats, Tools & Supplies

In addition to your actual cutting machine, there are many tools, supplies, and accessories that you might want to make your crafting easier.

Blades

You will have a wide variety of blades to choose from, depending on your cutting machine. Many of the projects in this book use a standard blade included with the machine. There are also wood and chipboard projects that require a knife/kraft blade, and fabric projects for which a rotary blade works best.

Cutting Mats

The cutting machine you have will dictate the cutting mats you can use. Mats generally come in several levels of "stickiness," such as light, standard, and strong. Most of the projects in this book require a standard mat, though I suggest a strong mat for wood and leather projects. Cricut also has a fabric mat, which you can use with their rotary blade, though I have found a standard mat works just as well. Most machines use both 12" x 12" and 12" x 24" mats—you'll see both used here.

Weeding Tool

A weeding tool or hook, which looks like a dental pick, is used for removing negative adhesive vinyl or iron-on vinyl from a project (the part of the project that isn't your design). A weeding tool is essential—trying to get rid of that excess vinyl is practically impossible without it. Some crafters use a large needle, but I find a weeding tool to be the best option. I also use the weeding tool when picking up glue dots as it keeps my fingers sticky-free.

Scraper

Use the scraper to clean your mat after cutting something with a lot of negative bits. I find it works best with paper, but it will work with other materials as well. I often put my mat over my thigh/knee and scrape the leftover paper directly into the trash can—the mat is flexible and can be scraped well without pulling up any part of the adhesive on the mat.

You can also use the scraper as a bone folder to get a crisp edge when folding on scored lines. The scraper doubles as a burnishing tool when using transfer tape, as you'll see in several projects.

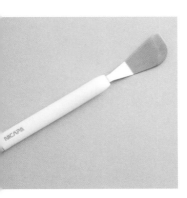

Spatula

The spatula is a must-have when you work with paper. If you are not careful, pulling the paper off a cutting mat may cause tearing or curling. The spatula is thin and slips easily under paper projects, allowing you to ease them off the mat carefully. See the next section in this book for more tips for removing materials from your mats.

Tweezers

A pair of tweezers is always handy for picking up small pieces in your projects. The Cricut fine-tipped tweezers are my most frequently used tool.

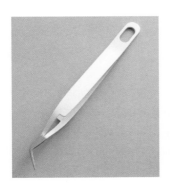
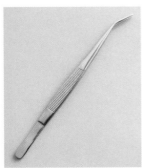

Brayer

A brayer, or hand roller, is used for improving adhesion between the material and the mat. It's good for eliminating wrinkles and bubbles in materials, including vinyl, iron-on vinyl, and fabric.

If your mat is coming toward the end of its life, place the material down on the mat and run the brayer over it—it will help it stick more firmly and evenly, extending the life of the mat.

Scissors

I have a wide range of scissors for different projects. My favorites include:

- Everyday use: Fiskars® Original Orange Handled 8" Scissors™
- Detail work: Olfa® Precision Smooth Edge 5" Scissors
- For use with felt: Havel's® Sewing Serrated 7" Fabric Scissors
- For use with fabric: Fiskars® RazorEdge™ 8" Fabric Shears

Flat-Nose Pliers

When making jewelry, flat-nose pliers are essential for opening and closing jump rings and jewelry findings.

Rotary Cutter, Acrylic Ruler, and Self-Healing Cutting Mat

Although the cutting machine will do the bulk of the cutting, I always have a rotary cutter, acrylic ruler, and self-healing cutting mat on my craft table.

I use these tools for trimming materials down to size or trimming off the unused portion of material after a cut. It allows for a straight, even cut when I use the remaining vinyl, for instance, in a future project.

Craft Knife

A craft knife is always handy to have around. I use mine for finishing cuts that haven't quite gone all the way through (this often happens in the corners of thicker materials like chipboard), and for quickly opening plastic-wrapped packs of materials.

Heating Tools

If you are going to be working with iron-on vinyl, you have several heating tool options for adhering the transfer. Following are the most common.

Household Iron

A household iron is the budget option for applying iron-on vinyl. However, household irons generally don't have precise heat settings, so you may want to do a test before working on your final project. For most iron-on vinyl projects, set your iron to cotton with no steam. On the plus side, an iron is lightweight, easy to store, and economical and can be used for other ironing tasks. Since you can't set an exact temperature and it may have hot and cold spots, I don't generally recommend an iron for most crafters.

Cricut EasyPress™

The Cricut EasyPress is a handheld heat press. Unlike an iron, the heating on the EasyPress is even from edge

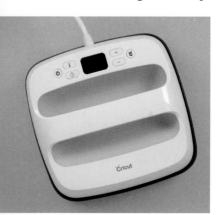

to edge, making it perfect for iron-on vinyl projects—no scorching. It's easy to use right out of the box, it's lighter than a traditional heat press, and it's easier to store. It comes in several sizes, which is great if you're working on a lot of iron-on projects. The Cricut EasyPress is my preferred tool—it is the best marriage between a household iron and a traditional heat press. You will see I use it for most of the projects in this book.

Cricut AutoPress™

The Cricut AutoPress is Cricut's version of a traditional heat press. This sleek and modern heat press automatically applies pressure to your project, making it very easy to use. It also has an automatic-open feature, which allows you to do other tasks while your project presses.

Traditional Heat Press

Many crafters swear by a heat press, and I understand why! Every time I've used mine, I've had a lot of success—iron-on vinyl adheres beautifully with it. It's not my favorite, however, primarily because a 40-pound heat press takes up valuable space in my small studio. If you love yours, by all means, use it.

Mini Iron or Cricut EasyPress Mini™

In addition to a larger heating tool, having a mini iron or Cricut EasyPress Mini is also handy in a craft room. A smaller heating tool is great for curved surfaces and tight places, and I have also found it works well when I'm struggling to get one particular area of my transfer to adhere properly. I have had success with both the Clover mini iron and the EasyPress Mini.

Pressing Mat

For most of the projects in this book, I suggest using a pressing mat instead of an ironing board. The ironing board will siphon off the heat from the press, making it less effective because the iron-on vinyl won't stick properly, which can be exasperating. The only time I recommend using an ironing board is with large projects,

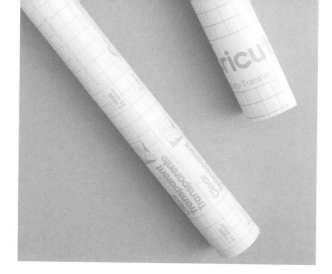

though you may need to increase press times to get good adherence.

I have a Cricut EasyPress mat (which I have used for the projects in this book) and a wool mat. I like and use both of them.

Teflon™ Sheet

When using iron-on vinyl, I often use a Teflon pressing sheet between my project and the heat press plate. Though it is not necessary for all projects, I find a Teflon sheet does prevent the plastic carrier sheet from warping as I press, giving me a cleaner final project. You can also use a piece of cotton fabric as a pressing cloth or nothing at all.

Transfer Tape

Transfer tape (sometimes called transfer paper) will transfer your design from the vinyl's carrier sheet to your project, keeping all the pieces of the vinyl in the correct position. There are many brands of transfer tape with varying stickiness levels, so you may need to try a few to find one you like. I prefer Craftopia transfer tape for most of my projects, but I also use Cricut StrongGrip transfer tape when working with difficult materials like glitter vinyl.

Adhesives

I have a whole cabinet in my studio devoted to glue! Here are a few that I always use:

- Double-sided adhesive roller: use with paper and cardstock

- Adhesive strips (Command™ picture-hanging strips): use with a variety of materials, and can be cut in half lengthwise to fit narrow projects

- Spray adhesive: use with paper and cardstock

- Hot glue gun: use with a huge variety of materials, including cardstock, wood, felt, and leather

- Glue stick: use with paper and cardstock

- E6000® Industrial Strength Adhesive: use with thicker materials such as wood and leather

- Xyron® Creative Station™: applies a sticker-like finish to the back of cardstock and other materials

- Heat-resistant tape: use to keep iron-on transfers in place while setting with a heat press or Cricut EasyPress.

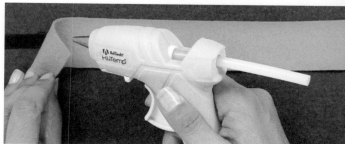

Cutting-Machine Materials

Now let's get to the good stuff and what this book is all about: cutting-machine materials! There are so many materials you can cut with your cutting machine, even if you're working with a basic model.

Although most of the projects in this book can be cut with any standard cutting machine, some of them will require specialized blades like a knife/kraft blade or rotary blade. The type of blade needed is listed in the supply list for each project.

Cardstock, Paper, and Chipboard

Some of my favorite materials to work with are cardstock and other papers. They are generally inexpensive and come in a dazzling array of colors, coatings, and patterns. For this book, I'm primarily using solid cardstock and

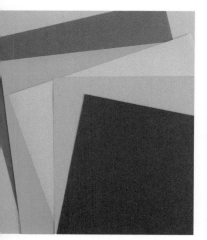

scrapbook paper, but your cutting machine will also cut glitter and foiled cardstock, wrapping paper, origami paper, and more. Customize the projects on the following pages as much as you'd like!

Cutting Cardstock and Paper

Cutting cardstock and paper is generally simple with any cutting machine. Choose a standard or light mat, place your paper down, and cut with a standard blade. If the paper shifts, use a brayer to secure it to the mat or get a new mat.

Removing paper from a cutting mat can be tricky, so make sure you read the helpful tips on page 23.

Cutting Chipboard

For a few of the projects in this book, I used thicker paper materials. Most craft cutting machines can cut kraft board with their standard blade, but you may need a machine with a knife blade to cut particularly thick materials like chipboard. Always follow the manufacturer's guidelines for cutting thick materials—you may need to tape them down to the mat to help secure them before cutting.

Iron-On Vinyl

Iron-on vinyl, also called heat-transfer vinyl or HTV, is backed with an adhesive that is activated by heat. It's great for T-shirts and other apparel, but it can also be used on a huge variety of base materials, including wood, cardstock, cork, and metal.

Cutting Iron-On Vinyl

There are two important things to do when cutting iron-on vinyl. First, "mirror" or "reverse" the image in the cutting machine software to ensure that the image is not backward when you iron it onto your base material. Second, place the shiny side of the iron-on vinyl down on the cutting mat. Use a standard mat and a standard blade, and the iron-on vinyl should cut perfectly.

Weeding Iron-On Vinyl

Once you've cut the iron-on vinyl, you will need to weed out the excess material that is not a part of your design, often called the "negative material." The easiest way to do this is by using a weeding hook—dig the hook into the excess vinyl and pull it up. For more complex designs, hold them up to the light to make sure you've weeded all of the small pieces from your project.

Adhering Iron-On Vinyl

You'll adhere the iron-on vinyl with a heating tool, like an iron, Cricut EasyPress, or heat press. You can read about my suggested heating tools on page 16.

Before you begin to press your project, check the suggested time and temperature of the specific iron-on vinyl. Most standard iron-on vinyl is applied with the "cotton" setting on an iron or 315°F on a Cricut EasyPress or heat press. Specialty materials, however, such as metallic and glitter iron-on, will have different settings. Always ensure you have the correct setting before you begin—it can make or break your project.

You will also want to check to see if your iron-on vinyl is "warm peel" or "cool peel." Most packages list it, but you can also look it up online. If the iron-on vinyl is warm peel, wait 15–30 seconds before you peel off the backing liner. If it is cool peel, wait until the project is completely cool before removing the backing liner.

If you are afraid your project might shift while you press, or if you need very precise placement, I recommend using heat-resistant tape. Use it to secure the iron-on vinyl transfer to the base material.

When adhering iron-on vinyl, avoid moving the heating tool around. Press firmly and hold for 20–30 seconds before moving to the next area. It's then easy to press images that are larger than your heating tool. If you are pressing a curved surface with a mini iron, however, move the heating tool around so you can cover the entire transfer. Should the liner piece not peel easily, press for 15 seconds more and try peeling it again.

The "Cut-Through" Technique

For several of the projects in this book, I'm using the "cut-through" technique. Instead of using the "iron-on vinyl" cut setting, use the "cardstock" cut setting. Your machine will cut through the entire carrier sheet, generating separate pieces. This method requires no weeding and works for projects with large pieces or those that do not require precise placement in relation to one another.

Wash and Care Instructions

Let the project cure for at least 24 hours before washing. Then, wash inside out and line dry to help preserve the iron-on vinyl transfer.

Adhesive Vinyl

Adhesive vinyl is an adhesive-backed material, much like a sticker. The best base surfaces for adhesive vinyl are smooth and nonporous, such as glass, plastic, or ceramics. Adhesive vinyl is also great for making wall decals—just make sure you choose removable, instead of permanent, adhesive vinyl. In this book I'm using a variety of solid

colors, but you can use any adhesive vinyl you'd like, including patterned, glitter, foil, and more.

Cutting Adhesive Vinyl

To cut adhesive vinyl, use a standard mat and blade. Place the adhesive vinyl liner side down on the mat.

Weeding Adhesive Vinyl

Like iron-on vinyl, most adhesive vinyl projects need to be weeded. The process is the same. Just dig the hook into the excess adhesive vinyl and pull it up.

Adhering Adhesive Vinyl

Most often, you'll use transfer tape to apply the vinyl to a project. Each tutorial in this book has instructions for doing so. You will need a burnishing tool or scraper, which you can learn more about on page 14.

A few of the projects do not require transfer tape—you'll peel up the cut pieces like stickers and place them on the base material (I love those projects—they're so easy!).

Felt

Felt is a popular material to cut with the cutting machine. You can use it to make all sorts of projects, from flowers for embroidery hoops to party decorations. I prefer using a wool blend felt instead of the acrylic felt you'll find at the craft store. It is thicker, feels more organic, cuts better, and produces a beautiful final project.

Cutting Felt

If your machine has a rotary blade, use it! The rolling motion of the blade slices through felt like butter. If not, you may need to use a multicut setting with a standard cutting blade to get through the fibrous material. If your cuts go only partially through the felt (often the corners will remain connected), you can use a pair of sharp scissors to finish the cut. For some projects, you can

also back the felt with a stabilizer—this helps keep the felt from tearing. Using a strong mat can help as well.

One option to help keep the cutting mat free of felt fibers is to back it with transfer tape. When cutting, place the felt with the transfer tape side down on the mat. After cutting, peel off the transfer tape. It works well with simple designs, but the felt may stretch and pull when you remove the transfer tape from more intricate cuts.

Another option is to keep your older, well-used mats for cutting felt. The mat should have enough "stick" to hold the felt, but not be so new as to be ruined by all the felt fibers sticking to it.

Wood

I love creating wood projects with my cutting machine—it has added variety to the types of projects I can make.

Through experience, I've learned that basswood works better than other woods like balsa. Basswood is less susceptible to breaking or splitting, it's more economical, it can be painted or stained, and it comes in large sheets. Cricut, for instance, makes an 11" x 11" sheet, which they designed to be cut by their Maker machine. I use basswood throughout this book.

Cutting Wood

Whether or not you can cut wood will depend on your cutting machine's capabilities. Generally, you will need a heavy-duty knife/kraft blade to cut through most types of wood. Always follow the manufacturer's instructions for cutting thicker materials—you may need to take several steps before cutting it, such as taping the material to the mat.

When cutting, a knife blade may leave little nicks in the corners of your cuts. The cleaner part of the cut will be the side facing down on the mat. If you reverse the image before you cut, the front of the project will end up being the cleaner cut.

If the majority of your project is cut through and just a few corners remain, eject the mat and finish the cuts with a craft knife.

Cork

When you're looking to add interest or texture, cork can be a fun option. It brings a natural element to your projects

and can work with many different design styles. But beware: not all cork is created equal. I have found that adhesive-backed cork cuts best on my cutting machine. Unbacked cork tends to fall apart either while cutting or while trying to remove it from the mat. Cork is best for simple shapes—intricate cuts may leave you frustrated.

Cutting Cork

I've had the best results cutting cork with a standard mat and a rotary cutting blade, with the adhesive side of the cork down on the mat. If the cork shifts, apply a little piece of tape around the edges to help keep it in place.

Fabric

My mom taught me how to sew when I was a young girl, and I've loved it ever since. So, when Cricut released the rotary blade for my cutting machine, I couldn't have been happier. Now, I can cut unbonded fabric for sewing projects! The rotary blade rolls over and slices through the fabric instead of dragging a blade over it to cut it. It leaves a clean, accurate cut, which is perfect for sewing patterns.

Most cutting machines with a rotary blade can cut an endless array of fabrics, from thicker materials like canvas and denim to delicate fabrics like silk and mesh. I've used cotton in this book, but your choices are limitless. You can even cut interfacing!

All of the fabric projects here are cut using a rotary blade, and all seams are ¼".

Cutting machines without a rotary blade may be able to cut bonded fabric (a fabric that has a stabilizer ironed to the back), using a standard blade. It is an option for some of the more stable projects I designed, such as the tote bag and fabric bins, but would not work as well for the quilt or fabric tassels.

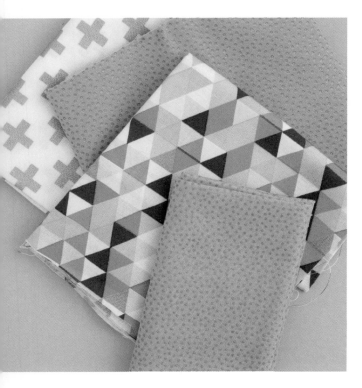

Genuine and Faux Leather

Leather is another material that has an organic feel—it works well for jewelry, fashion projects, and home décor ideas. Both genuine and faux leather come in an assortment of different colors and textures to match any style. I love working with these two types of leather—the choice of one or the other ultimately depends on the project. I've used both in this book!

Most cutting machines can cut genuine and faux leather. You may need a deep-cut or knife blade for thicker leathers. The leather projects in this book, however, can all be cut using a standard blade or a rotary blade. I generally prefer the rotary blade for how smoothly it cuts.

Cutting Leather

To cut both genuine and faux leather, use a strong mat and a rotary blade or standard blade. Place the leather facedown on the mat and secure it with tape on the sides if you think it might shift. You can also use a brayer to really press the leather into the mat's adhesive, giving you more grip.

Cutting Fabric

For cutting unbonded fabric, use a rotary blade and either a fabric or standard mat. I recommend using a brayer to help adhere the fabric to the cutting mat.

When the machine cutting is finished, you may barely see the cut marks. As you peel the excess fabric away, though, you'll see that it has cut your pieces perfectly. Use tweezers to help lift the fabric pieces off the mat without stretching them.

If your mat ends up covered in threads, don't worry. Place the next piece of fabric right on top, and the rotary blade will cut through it all.

Tips & Tricks

Uploading SVG Files

All of the projects in this book require you to upload SVG files to your cutting machine software. The process for this is different with each software, so refer to the manufacturer's guide for instructions.

Changing Cut Lines to Score Lines

Because it's impossible to design a file with a score line outside the design software, several projects will require you to change cut lines to score lines, as noted in the tutorials. As this process is different for every software, refer to the manufacturer's guide for how to do it.

Making the Most of Your Materials

Some design software programs allow you to move images around on the mat layout to use the materials more efficiently. I suggest getting to know this feature of your cutting machine software—it can save you time and money in the long run!

Removing Materials off the Mat

When I got my Cricut, I decided my first project would be to cut out my logo in paper. My brand-new Explore cut it beautifully. I was so impressed looking at it on the green mat. And then, I tried to remove my delicate logo from it.

It was a disaster. It ripped and curled and stuck to the mat, ruining my project. Don't let this happen to you! Here are some important tips for removing materials off your cutting mat.

Prime the Mat

When you first open your mat, instead of using it right away, pat the sticky side against your shirt a little. It will pick up the lint and prime it somewhat, easing the removal of your project.

Use Your Tools

When I did my first project, I had no way of carefully lifting that delicate paper from the mat. Now I use the spatula to pry up delicate projects. The tweezers are also helpful to grip tiny pieces. You can read more about these and other helpful tools starting on page 14.

Bend the Mat

Instead of peeling your project up off the mat, bend the mat in your hand both horizontally and vertically, letting the adhesive move, and curve it away from the material to help loosen it. Use the spatula—never grab your work by the corner and try to lift it, since it will tear or curl.

Go Slowly. Go Carefully. Breathe.

Sometimes, the best thing you can do to get an intricate cut off the mat is to go slowly. I tend to start slowly and then rush toward the end—usually, that's when things go downhill. Trust me—taking your time will save you a lot of hassle!

+++++++++++++++++++++++++

Home

Add a handmade touch to your home with these unique home décor ideas! Choose the projects that speak to you, personalize them with colors that match your décor, and follow the steps to make them your own. You'll be able to tell your family and friends, "I made this!" These projects are also great as holiday and housewarming gifts.

+++++++++++++++++++++++++++++++

Paper Quilt Wall Art

You don't need sewing skills to make these paper quilt blocks! Just cut the triangles from a rainbow of cardstock and glue them together. I used two 18" square frames from a thrift store spray-painted navy blue.

SUPPLIES & MATERIALS

- Standard cutting blade
- 12" x 12" standard cutting mat
- 2 square frames with white backing board
- 2 sheets of white cardstock, 12" x 12"
- 2 sheets of light pink cardstock, 12" x 12"
- 1 sheet of medium pink cardstock, 12" x 12"
- 1 sheet of dark pink cardstock, 12" x 12"
- 1 sheet of yellow cardstock, 12" x 12"
- 2 sheets of light blue cardstock, 12" x 12"
- 1 sheet of medium blue cardstock, 12" x 12"
- 1 sheet of teal cardstock, 12" x 12"
- 1 sheet of navy blue cardstock, 12" x 12"
- Spray adhesive
- Paper Quilt Wall Art SVG file

BEFORE YOU BEGIN

- Supplies and instructions are for making two pieces of artwork.
- For more information on cutting cardstock, see page 18.
- Resize the blocks in your cutting machine software as needed for the size of your frames.

INSTRUCTIONS

1. Cut the cardstock pieces.

2. Glue the pieces to the backing board of the frame using spray adhesive, as shown in the diagrams.

3. If your frame is not quite plumb, you may need to trim a few pieces slightly to get a perfect fit. I find that a rotary cutter and an acrylic ruler are perfect for this.

Diagrams

Plus Sign Wall Decals

A little removable adhesive vinyl goes a long way to create "wallpaper"! This project is perfect for spaces where you don't want to put a permanent wall treatment—just peel it off the wall to remove.

SUPPLIES & MATERIALS

- Standard cutting blade
- 12" x 12" standard cutting mat
- 4 pieces of black removable adhesive vinyl, 12" x 12"
- Weeding tool (optional)
- Plus Sign Wall Decal SVG **file**

BEFORE YOU BEGIN

- Supplies and instructions are for making enough decals for an 8' x 10' wall.
- For more information on cutting adhesive vinyl, see page 20.
- The pieces are large enough that you do not need to use transfer tape. Just pick up a piece as you would any other sticker and adhere it to the wall.
- You can map out a grid on the wall or place the plus signs randomly.

INSTRUCTIONS

1. Cut the adhesive vinyl pieces.
2. Weed out the excess material (this is optional, but it makes it easier to pick up each piece).
3. Peel up the plus sign pieces by hand and place them on the wall.

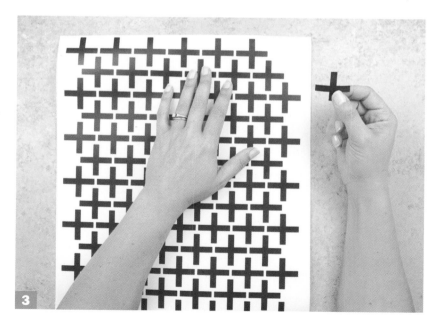

+++++++++++++++++++++++++++++++++

Tiny House Pillows

Turn your house into "home sweet home" with these adorable pillows, plus practice layering iron-on vinyl. The black outline of these houses would also be perfect on large wood blocks as décor or applied to hand towels as a housewarming gift.

SUPPLIES & MATERIALS

- Rotary and standard cutting blade
- 12" x 24" and 12" x 12" fabric and standard cutting mats
- 6 pieces of white cotton fabric, 12" x 24"
- 1 piece of black iron-on vinyl, 12" x 24"
- 1 piece of black iron-on vinyl, 12" x 12"
- 1 piece of pink iron-on vinyl, 5" x 12"
- 1 piece of green iron-on vinyl, 2" x 12"
- 1 piece of teal iron-on vinyl, 5" x 12"
- Weeding tool
- Iron or Cricut EasyPress
- Pressing mat
- Teflon sheet or pressing cloth
- Heat-resistant tape
- Sewing machine and sewing supplies
- Polyester fiberfill stuffing
- Tiny House Pillows SVG file

BEFORE YOU BEGIN

- Supplies and instructions are for making three pillows.
- For more information on cutting standard iron-on vinyl, see page 18.
- For more information on cutting iron-on vinyl with the cut-through technique, see page 19.
- If your machine does not have a rotary blade, you can cut the fabric house shapes by hand—just make them an inch larger than the black house pieces.
- For more information on heat settings, see page 19.
- When layering iron-on vinyl, use only 20 seconds of press time for each of the layers—it will keep the iron-on vinyl from scorching.
- All seams are ¼".

INSTRUCTIONS

1. Cut the white fabric pieces.

2. Cut the black iron-on vinyl pieces using the iron-on vinyl setting.

3. Cut through the colored iron-on vinyl pieces using the cardstock setting.

4. Weed out the black negative material.

5. Lay a fabric house shape onto the pressing mat and prepress it with the heating tool for 15 seconds.

6. Center the coordinating house piece on the fabric.

7. Place a Teflon sheet or pressing cloth on top of the project.

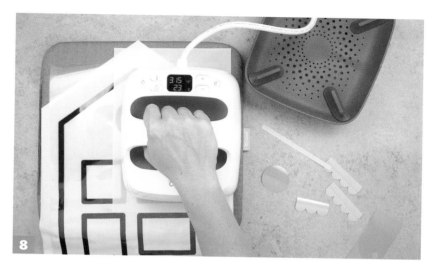

8. Following the manufacturer's instructions, use the iron or EasyPress to adhere the vinyl to the fabric, pressing from the back as necessary.

9. Peel off the plastic liner.

10. Position the colored vinyl pieces on the project. Use the heat-resistant tape to secure them.

11. Place the Teflon sheet or pressing cloth back on top of the project.

12. Following the manufacturer's instructions, use the iron or EasyPress to adhere the vinyl to the fabric, pressing from the back as necessary.

13. Peel off the plastic liners.

14. Place the house piece and the matching fabric piece right sides together and stitch all four sides, leaving a 3" gap at the bottom for turning.

15. Clip the corners.

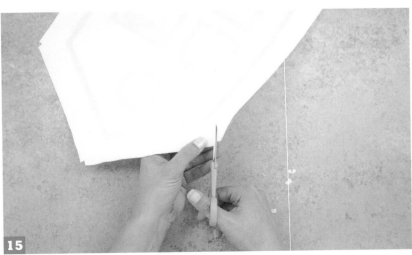

16. Turn the pillow right side out.

17. Stuff and hand-stitch the bottom closed.

18. Repeat this same process with the other two pillows.

+++++++++++++++++++++++++++++++

"Let's Stay In" Wood Sign

Painted signs are a favorite of cutting machine crafters, but working with stencils—particularly large stencils—can be challenging. Instead, I love using iron-on vinyl on wood to create the look of a stenciled sign without any of the headaches. I am using a 12" x 36" sign, with the frame spray painted pink.

Once you've made this sign, resize the cut file and use it on a nightshirt or pillow!

SUPPLIES & MATERIALS

- Standard cutting blade
- 12" x 24" standard cutting mat
- Wood frame with white backing board
- 1 piece of black iron-on vinyl, 12" x 24"
- Weeding tool
- Mini iron or Cricut EasyPress Mini
- Pressing mat
- Teflon sheet or pressing cloth
- Ruler (optional)
- "Let's Stay In" Wood Sign SVG file

BEFORE YOU BEGIN

- Supplies and instructions are for making one sign.
- A mini iron works best for wood. It's particularly helpful if the wood is not perfectly flat, as it can heat into the dips and imperfections of the wood better than the larger heating plate of a standard iron or heating press.
- For more information on cutting standard iron-on vinyl, see page 18.
- For more information on heat settings, see page 19.

INSTRUCTIONS

1. Cut the iron-on vinyl pieces.

2. Weed out the negative material.

3. Place the frame on the pressing mat.

4. Lay the iron-on vinyl pieces on the backing board of the frame. You may want to use a ruler to make sure they are straight.

5. Layer a Teflon sheet or pressing cloth on top of the project.

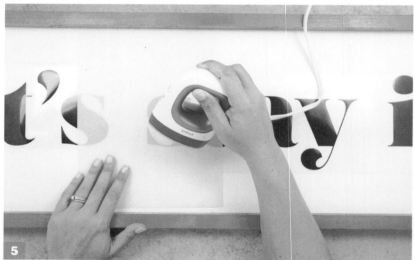

6. Following the manufacturer's instructions, use the mini iron or EasyPress to adhere the vinyl to the sign, moving the iron or press around so it doesn't scorch.

7. Peel off the plastic liner. If it does not peel easily, press again.

let's stay in

Terrazzo Vase

Terrazzo has made a serious comeback in recent years, generally with clay projects. To get this look with a cutting machine, I'm using adhesive vinyl and a 14" geometric vase. This project is very forgiving—just cut more shapes in adhesive vinyl and continue to add until you get the look you like. It's also a great scrap-busting project!

SUPPLIES & MATERIALS

- Standard cutting blade
- 12" x 12" standard cutting mat
- 1 white vase
- Alcohol wipes
- 1 piece of black adhesive vinyl, 3" x 12"
- 1 piece of gray adhesive vinyl, 3" x 12"
- 1 piece of light pink adhesive vinyl, 3" x 12"
- 1 piece of dark pink adhesive vinyl, 3" x 12"
- 1 piece of yellow adhesive vinyl, 3" x 12"
- Weeding tool
- Terrazzo Vase SVG file

BEFORE YOU BEGIN

- Supplies and instructions are for making one vase.
- You do not need to use transfer tape for this project. Just pick up a piece of vinyl like a sticker and adhere it to the vase.

INSTRUCTIONS

1. Clean the vase with alcohol wipes.

2. Cut the adhesive vinyl pieces.

3. Weed out the negative material.

4. Stick the shapes on the vase by hand until you achieve a look you love.

Flower Coasters

Protect your coffee table and add style to a room with a customized set of coasters! Pick any permanent adhesive vinyl to match your décor. These Scandinavian-inspired cut files are versatile—put these flowers on anything from tote bags to wall art to notebooks.

SUPPLIES & MATERIALS

- ■ Standard cutting blade
- ■ 12" x 12" standard cutting mat
- ■ Set of 4 coasters
- ■ Alcohol wipes
- ■ 1 piece of pink adhesive vinyl, 4" x 4"
- ■ 1 piece of yellow adhesive vinyl, 4" x 4"
- ■ 1 piece of teal adhesive vinyl, 4" x 4"
- ■ 1 piece of navy blue adhesive vinyl, 4" x 4"
- ■ Weeding tool
- ■ 4 pieces of transfer tape, 4" x 4"
- ■ Burnishing tool
- ■ Flower Coasters SVG file

BEFORE YOU BEGIN

- ■ Supplies and instructions are for making four 3½" coasters.
- ■ For more information on cutting adhesive vinyl, see page 20.

INSTRUCTIONS

1. Clean the coasters with alcohol wipes.

2. Cut the adhesive vinyl pieces.

3. Weed out the negative material.

4. Peel back the transfer tape liner and place the transfer tape top on the first flower.

5. Burnish to press the transfer tape onto the vinyl.

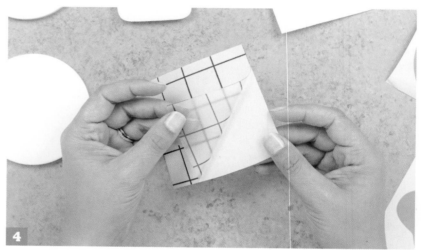

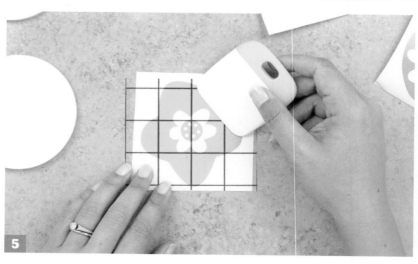

6. Peel back the liner from the vinyl. The flower should stick to the transfer tape.

7. Place the flower on the coaster.

8. Burnish to press the flower onto the coaster.

9. Peel back the transfer tape. The flower should stick to the coaster.

10. Repeat with the remaining coasters.

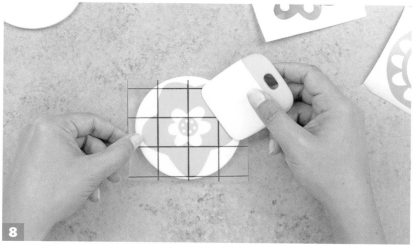

Modern Felt Flower Wreath

Felt flowers have become a staple in my studio—they are so fun to make! In this project, I'm using them to make a modern flower wreath using a large brass ring. These flowers are also lovely on headbands and hair clips, in faux flower bouquets, and more.

SUPPLIES & MATERIALS

- Rotary or standard cutting blade
- 12" x 12" standard cutting mat
- 1 piece of gray felt, 5" x 12"
- 1 piece of black felt, 2" x 12"
- 3 pieces of off-white felt, 9" x 12"
- 2 pieces of pink felt, 9" x 12"
- 1 piece of yellow felt, 9" x 12"
- 1 piece of green felt for leaves, 5" x 12"
- 1 strip of green felt for wrapping the ring, 2" x 15"
- 6 off-white ¾" felt balls
- 1 black 1" felt ball
- 19" metal wreath ring
- Hot glue gun
- Modern Felt Flower Wreath SVG file

BEFORE YOU BEGIN

- Supplies and instructions are for making one wreath.
- For more information on cutting felt, see page 20.
- For this wreath, cut the following flowers:
  - One large off-white anemone (use with the 2.5cm black felt ball)
  - Two small off-white anemones (use with the 2cm off-white felt balls)
  - Two large pink peonies (use with the 2cm off-white felt balls)
  - Two small pink peonies (use with the 2cm off-white felt balls)
  - Three yellow dandelions
  - Three large green leaves
  - Three small green leaves
  - One black fringe strip
  - One long and two short gray fringe strips

INSTRUCTIONS

1. Cut the felt pieces as listed on page 51.

Anemones

2. To make the anemones:

   - Glue the fringe strip(s) around the felt ball. The large anemone has two strips, and the small anemone has only one (a, b, c, d, e).

   - Glue the first set of five petals to the center of the flower, aligning the base of the petal with the bottom of the fringe strip (f, g, h).

   - Glue the second set of five petals to the outside of the first set to finish the anemone (i, j).

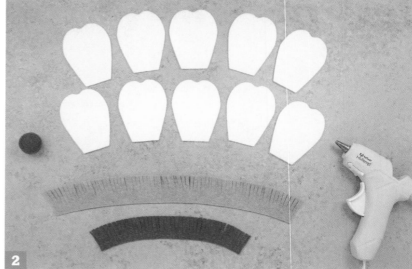

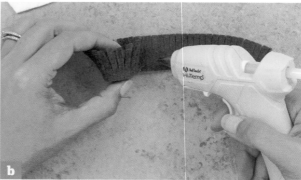

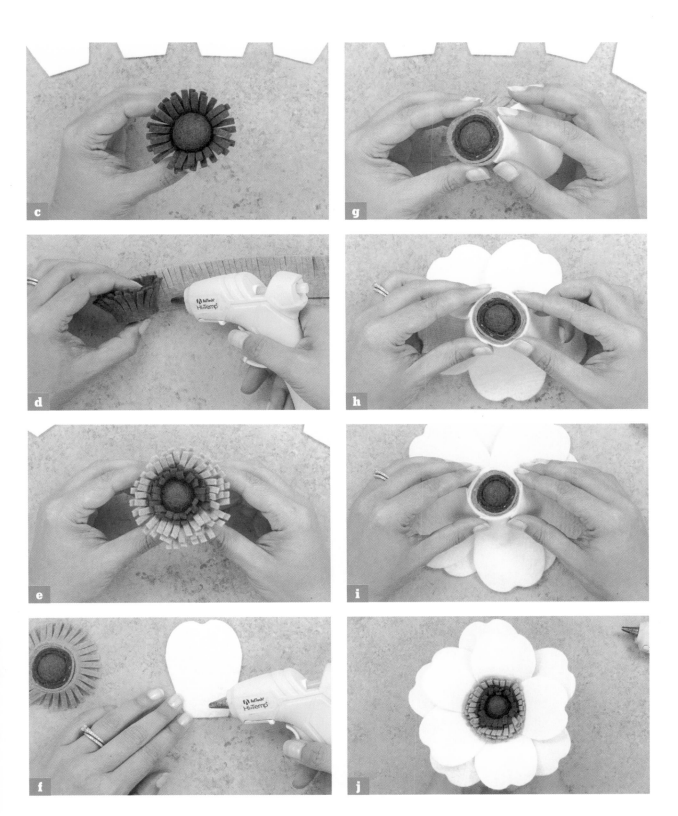

Dandelions

3. To make the dandelions:

- Stack the two pieces with the taller, shorter piece on top (a).

- Place a line of glue along the base and roll to create the flower (b, c, d).

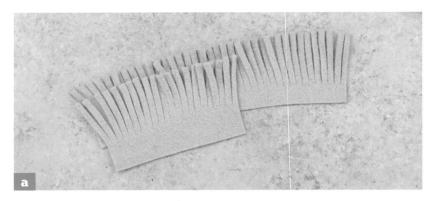

a

b

c

d

Peonies

4. To make the peonies:

   - Glue the flower piece around the felt ball, keeping the bottom edge aligned all the way around (a, b).

   - Glue the flap to the bottom to finish the peony (c, d, e).

Wreath Assembly

5. Wrap the strip of green felt around the wreath, gluing as you go to secure it (a, b, c).

6. Glue the large anemone to the center of the felt strip (d, e).

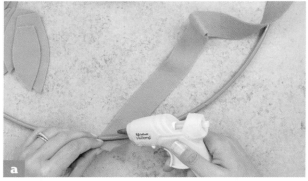

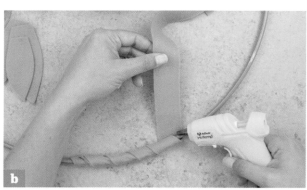

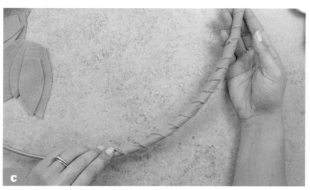

7. Glue the two small anemones on both sides of the large anemone (f).

8. Add the dandelions and peonies (g, h).

9. Finish the wreath by adding the leaves (i).

Cork Leaf Planters

Layer organic materials like concrete and cork to create these unique planters. The simple leaf cut files can be used in so many ways: with iron-on vinyl on hand towels, with adhesive vinyl on a vase, or with felt to make a beautiful wreath. They are an easy way to bring the outdoors in!

SUPPLIES & MATERIALS

- Rotary cutting blade
- 12" x 12" standard cutting mat
- 2 concrete planters
- 1 piece of adhesive-backed cork, 12" x 12"
- Cork Leaf Planters SVG file

BEFORE YOU BEGIN

- Supplies and instructions are for making two planters.
- For more information on cutting cork, see page 21.

INSTRUCTIONS

1. If your software does not have Cork under "Materials," set it to Denim. Cut the cork pieces.

2. Remove the backing and adhere the cork pieces to the planters.

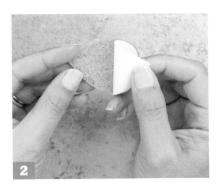

Plus Sign Quilt

One of the more innovative features of many cutting machines is the rotary blade. This blade makes sewing projects, like this 47¼" x 57¾" quilt, a breeze! It is perfect for beginners—I've designed it so you don't have to line up any seams, making it delightfully forgiving for crafters new to a sewing machine.

SUPPLIES & MATERIALS

- Rotary cutting blade
- 12" x 24" fabric or standard cutting mat
- ½ yard pink fabric
- ½ yard yellow fabric
- ½ yard light blue fabric
- ½ yard navy blue fabric
- ⅝ yard black fabric for binding
- 2¼ yards white fabric
- 3½ yards backing fabric
- 55" x 67" piece of batting
- Sewing machine and supplies
- Rotary cutter, rotary cutting mat, and rotary cutting ruler to cut fabric strips and squares (optional)
- Plus Sign Quilt SVG file

BEFORE YOU BEGIN

- Supplies and instructions are for making one quilt, including the backing and binding.
- For more information on cutting fabric, see page 22.
- All seams are ¼".

INSTRUCTIONS

1. Cutting three strips across the width of the fabric (from selvage to selvage), cut the white fabric into eight 12" x 24" strips. Cut the pink, yellow, light blue, and navy blue fabrics into one 12" x 24" strip and one 12" x 12" square.

2. Using the SVG file, cut the fabric pieces. You will get:

   - From white: (12) 5¾" squares, (7) 5¾" x 16¼" rectangles, and (12) 5¾" x 11" rectangles

   - From pink and light blue: (5) 5¾" squares and (2) 5¾" x 16¼" rectangles

   - From yellow and navy blue: (4) 5¾" squares and (2) 5¾" x 16¼" rectangles

3. Lay out the fabric pieces according to diagram 1. Sew them together in rows and press the seam allowances in one direction.

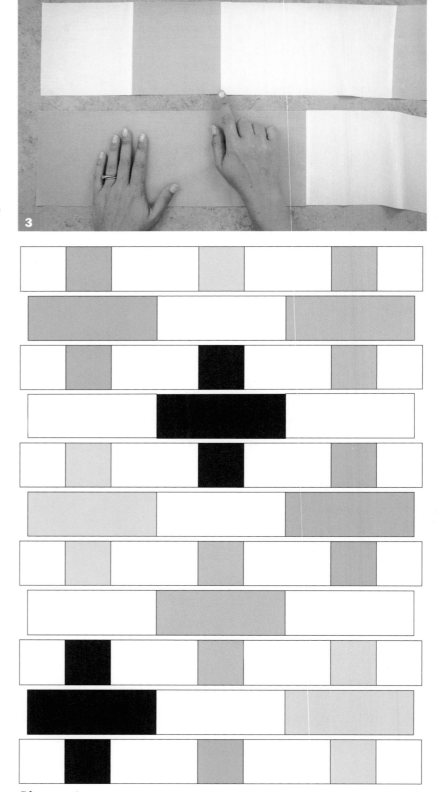

Diagram 1

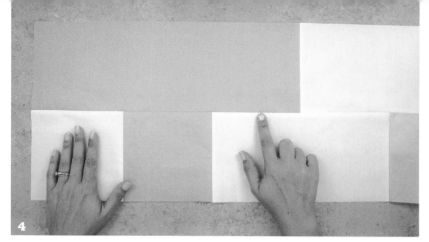

4. Sew the rows together to make the quilt top as outlined in diagram 2 and press the seam allowances in one direction.

Diagram 2

5. Cut the backing fabric in half across the width of the fabric (selvage to selvage). Sew the long edges together to make the quilt backing.

6. Layer the quilt top, batting, and backing and quilt as desired.

7. Cut the black binding fabric into six 2½" strips.

8. Stitch the binding strips together end to end using diagonal seams. Fold and press the resulting long strip in half lengthwise with the wrong sides together. Stitch it to the quilt front, matching raw edges and mitering the corners.

9. Fold the binding to the quilt underside and hand-stitch the folded edge to the quilt back.

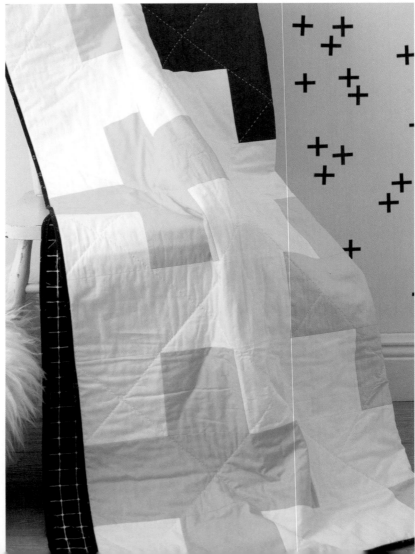

Decorative Jars

Store your bathroom essentials like cotton balls, cotton swabs, bobby pins, and hair ties in these beautiful and practical decorative jars.

SUPPLIES & MATERIALS

- Standard cutting blade
- 12" x 24" standard cutting mat
- 2 ceramic jars
- Alcohol wipes
- 1 piece of black adhesive vinyl, 3" x 13"
- 1 piece of pink adhesive vinyl, 3" x 18"
- 1 piece of transfer tape, 3" x 13"
- 1 piece of transfer tape, 3" x 18"
- Weeding tool
- Burnishing tool
- Decorative Jars SVG file

BEFORE YOU BEGIN

- Supplies and instructions are for making two jars.
- For more information on cutting adhesive vinyl, see page 20.
- Measure the diameter of the jars and calculate the circumference, then resize the cut file as needed to fit.

INSTRUCTIONS

1. Prepare the jars by wiping them with alcohol wipes.

2. Cut the adhesive vinyl pieces.

3. Weed out the negative material.

4. Peel back the liner from the transfer tape and place it on the vinyl.

5. Burnish to press the transfer tape onto the vinyl.

6. Peel back the transfer tape and the vinyl should stick to it.

7. Place the vinyl on the jar.

8. Using your fingers, burnish to press the vinyl onto the jar.

9. Peel back the transfer tape. The vinyl should stick to the jar.

10. Repeat with the remaining jar.

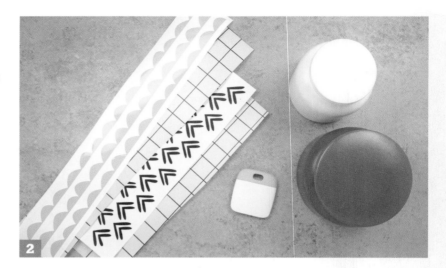

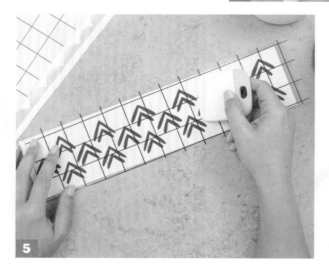

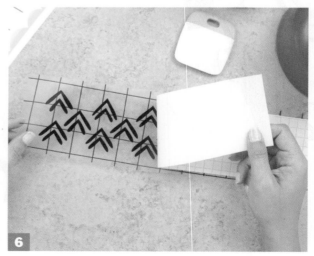

Leather Catchall Tray

This petite genuine leather tray is a must-have to keep the nightstand tidy. Use it for loose change, earrings, hair ties, and more. As a bonus, it unsnaps and stores flat.

SUPPLIES & MATERIALS

- Rotary standard cutting blade
- 12" x 12" strong cutting mat
- 1 piece of genuine leather, 8" x 8"
- 4 snap sets, 12.5mm
- Snap installation kit: anvil, punch tool, convex tool, and concave tool
- Hammer
- Small scrap of fabric
- Catchall Tray SVG file

BEFORE YOU BEGIN

- Supplies and instructions are for making one catchall tray.
- For more information on cutting genuine leather, see page 22.
- I have not found a cutting machine that can cut very small holes in genuine leather very well, so I used the punch that comes with the snap installation kit. The SVG file, however, has holes—run some test cuts and see if it works with your machine.

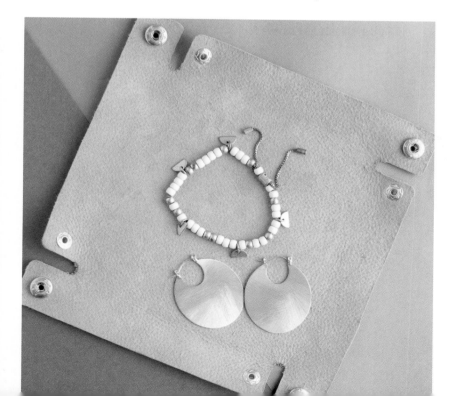

INSTRUCTIONS

1. Cut the leather piece.

2. Use the punch to create the first set of holes in the flaps, ½" from each edge.

3. Use the punch to create the second set of holes in the sides, ⅜" from the flap edge.

4. Using the convex tool and a hammer, install the cap and socket with the cap on the right side of the leather. Use a scrap of fabric between the cap and the anvil to protect it from scratches.

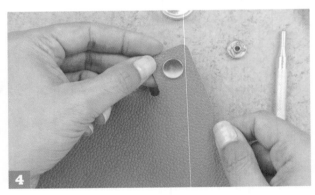

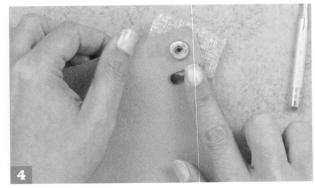

5. Using the concave tool and a hammer, install the post and stud with the stud on the right side of the leather. Use a scrap of fabric between the post and the anvil to protect it from scratches.

6. Snap all four sides to form the tray.

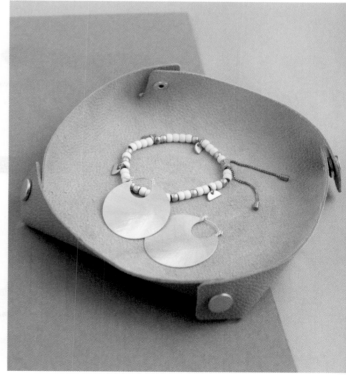

Earring Holder

Easily see your entire collection with this embroidery hoop earring holder. I love it with this diamond decoration, but you can use any number of cut files from this book—leaves, rainbows, flowers, and more.

SUPPLIES & MATERIALS

- Rotary or standard cutting blade
- 12" x 12" standard cutting mat
- 9" embroidery hoop
- 1 piece of gray felt, 11" x 11"
- 1 piece of teal felt, 7" x 7"
- 1 piece of light blue felt, 5" x 6"
- Basting spray
- Sewing machine and sewing supplies
- Earring Holder SVG file

BEFORE YOU BEGIN

- Supplies and instructions are for making one earring holder.
- For more information on cutting felt, see page 20.
- To help keep the felt from shifting as you sew, try a little basting spray. It works like a charm!

INSTRUCTIONS

1. Cut the pieces from felt.

2. Use basting spray to secure the teal diamond to the center of the gray felt, and stitch it down.

3. Use basting spray to secure the light blue diamond pieces to the teal diamond, and stitch them down.

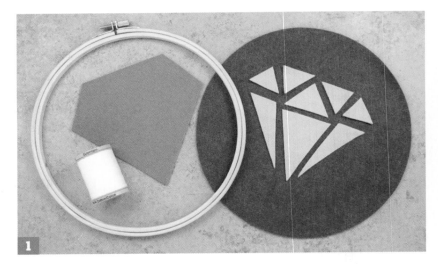

4. Lay the felt work over the inner ring of the embroidery hoop, place the outer ring over the felt and inner ring, and secure tightly.

Fabric Bins

Fabric bins are great for all sorts of bits and bobs. Use them in your closet for scarves, in the craft room for thread or ribbon, or in the kids' room for all those tiny toys that don't have a home.

SUPPLIES & MATERIALS

- ▪ Rotary cutting blade
- ▪ 12" x 24" fabric or standard cutting mat
- ▪ 1 piece of print fabric for the shell, 12" x 21"
- ▪ 1 piece of print fabric for the lining, 12" x 21"
- ▪ 1 piece of fusible fleece, 12" x 21"
- ▪ Iron
- ▪ Pressing mat or ironing board
- ▪ Sewing machine and sewing supplies
- ▪ Fabric Bins SVG file

BEFORE YOU BEGIN

- ▪ Supplies and instructions are for making one fabric bin.
- ▪ For more information on cutting fabric, see page 22.
- ▪ I chose fusible fleece to give shape to the bins. You can use the interfacing of your choice, depending on how stiff you want the bins.
- ▪ All seams are ¼".

INSTRUCTIONS

1. Cut the fabric and fusible fleece pieces.

2. Iron the fusible fleece to the shell fabric.

3. Fold the shell fabric and sew the sides and bottom.

4. Fold the lining fabric and sew the sides and bottom, leaving a 3" gap for turning.

5. Pinch the bottom corners of the shell and lining so that they create a box shape, and sew them closed.

6. Turn the lining right side out and nestle it within the shell, aligning the seams.

7. Sew around the top edge.

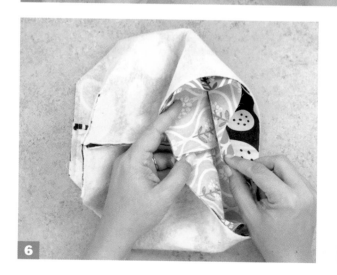

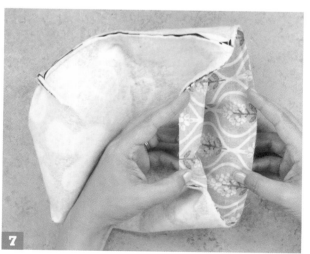

8. Pull the shell through the gap in the lining.

9. Hand-stitch the gap shut.

10. Press the top edge and topstitch all the way around.

11. Fold the top over 1" to complete the bin.

▲▲▲▲▲▲▲▲▲▲▲▲▲

Style

Make a fashion statement with these stylish clothing and accessory projects! You'll find both dressy and casual projects, including a flirty skirt, handmade jewelry, a comfortable hoodie, and a tote for all the essentials.

Layered Felt Necklace

Felt goes glam with this gorgeous layered necklace. Glitter felt is a sparkly alternative to its more natural wool-blend cousin. Finish with a velvet ribbon, and it's the perfect accessory for a night out on the town!

SUPPLIES & MATERIALS

- Rotary or standard cutting blade
- 12" x 12" standard cutting mat
- 1 piece of black glitter felt, 9" x 12"
- 1 piece of pink glitter felt, 9" x 12"
- 1 piece of gold glitter felt, 9" x 12"
- Hot glue gun
- 2 pieces of black velvet ribbon, 12" each
- Layered Felt Necklace SVG file

BEFORE YOU BEGIN

- Supplies and instructions are for making one necklace.
- For more information on cutting felt, see page 20.

INSTRUCTIONS

1. Cut the felt pieces.

2. Adhere the felt pieces using hot glue.

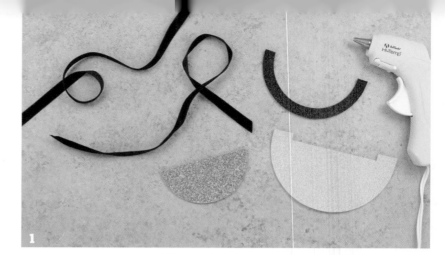

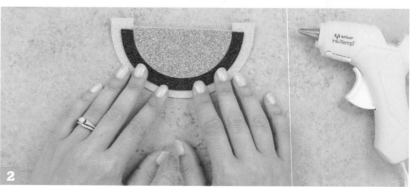

3. Thread a piece of ribbon through the slit at the top of the necklace.

4. Secure the ribbon with hot glue on the underside. Repeat with the other side.

5. Tie at the center back when ready to wear.

Cork Earrings

Cork is another in a long line of materials that work well with iron-on vinyl! I'm dressing up a pair of cork earrings with pink iron-on vinyl.

SUPPLIES & MATERIALS

- Rotary cutting blade
- 12" x 12" standard cutting mat
- 1 piece of adhesive-backed cork, 3" x 5"
- 1 piece of pink cardstock, 3" x 5"
- 1 piece of pink iron-on vinyl, 3" x 5"
- Weeding tool
- Iron or Cricut EasyPress
- Pressing mat
- Teflon sheet or pressing cloth
- Piercing tool
- 2 fishhook earring findings
- Flat-nose pliers
- Cork Earrings SVG file

BEFORE YOU BEGIN

- Supplies and instructions are for making one pair of earrings.
- Because the cork is a thinner material, backing the earrings with cardstock keeps them from curling.
- For more information on cutting cork, see page 21.
- For more information on cutting cardstock, see page 18.
- For more information on cutting iron-on vinyl, see page 18.
- For more information on heat settings, see page 19.

INSTRUCTIONS

1. Cut the cork, cardstock, and iron-on vinyl pieces.

2. Weed the negative material from the iron-on vinyl.

3. Remove the backing and adhere the cork to the cardstock. Place the cork earrings on the pressing mat.

4. Position the iron-on vinyl pieces on the earrings.

5. Layer a Teflon sheet or pressing cloth on top of the pieces.

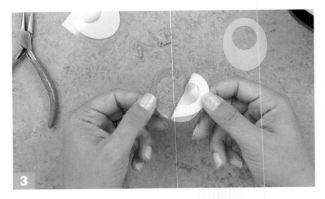

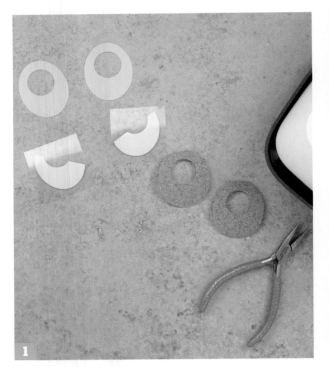

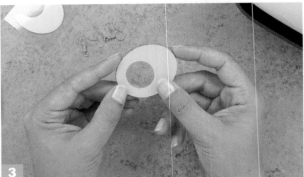

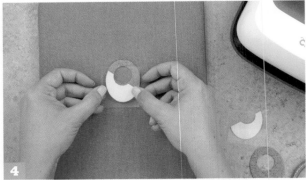

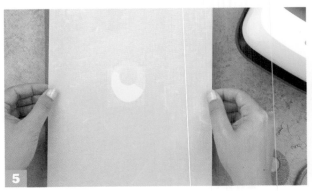

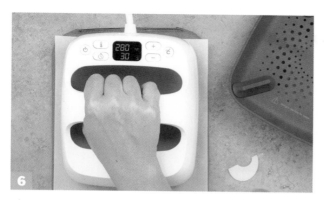

6. Following the manufacturer's instructions, use the iron or EasyPress to adhere the vinyl to the project.

7. Peel off the plastic liner.

8. Use the piercing tool to poke a small hole at the top of each earring.

9. Use the pliers to open the rings of the fishhook earrings and thread them through the holes on the earrings. Clamp closed.

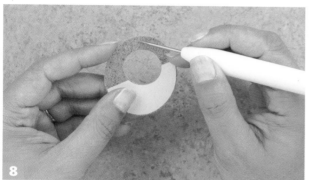

▲▲▲▲▲▲▲▲▲▲▲▲▲▲▲▲▲▲▲▲▲▲▲▲▲

Triangle Confetti Skirt

With a little iron-on vinyl, you can customize a basic skirt for any occasion! For this project, I'm using a store-bought skirt and light pink iron-on vinyl in a confetti triangle pattern—it's perfect for a party! Use this cut file on the bottom of a T-shirt or even as part of party décor.

SUPPLIES & MATERIALS

- ▇ Standard cutting blade
- ▇ 12" x 24" standard cutting mat
- ▇ Black skirt
- ▇ 2 pieces of light pink iron-on vinyl, 12" x 24"
- ▇ Weeding tool
- ▇ Iron or Cricut EasyPress
- ▇ Pressing mat or ironing board
- ▇ Teflon sheet or pressing cloth
- ▇ Triangle Confetti Skirt SVG file

BEFORE YOU BEGIN

- ▇ Supplies and instructions are for making one skirt.
- ▇ For more information on cutting iron-on vinyl, see page 18.
- ▇ You will need to work in sections. An ironing board is a good option for this project.
- ▇ Depending on the size and arc of the bottom of your skirt, you may need to trim the image as you go around.
- ▇ For more information on heat settings, see page 19.

INSTRUCTIONS

1. Cut the iron-on vinyl pieces.

2. Weed out the negative material.

3. Cut along the blank curved space between the bottom and the top of the transfer, separating it into two pieces.

4. Place your skirt on the table and place your pressing mat inside the skirt.

5. Position the image on the skirt.

6. Layer a Teflon sheet or pressing cloth on top of the piece.

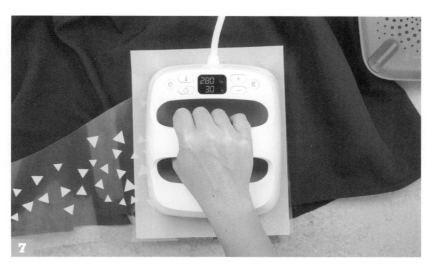

7. Following the manufacturer's instructions, use the iron or EasyPress to adhere the vinyl to the project.

8. Peel off the plastic liner.

9. Repeat with the rest of the skirt.

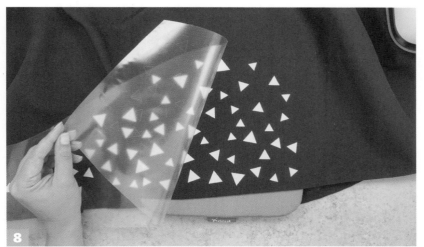

Leather Rings

Create comfortable leather rings in less than five minutes! I suggest using faux leather or faux suede, which are thinner than genuine leather and work nicely for this project.

SUPPLIES & MATERIALS

- Rotary or standard cutting blade
- 12" x 12" strong cutting mat
- 1 piece of black faux leather, 2" x 4"
- 1 piece of pink faux leather, 2" x 4"
- Leather Rings SVG file

BEFORE YOU BEGIN

- Supplies and instructions are for making two rings.
- For more information on cutting faux leather, see page 22.
- Cut in paper first to test the ring size. Need to adjust? Change the width in increments of 0.1".

INSTRUCTIONS

1. Cut the faux leather pieces.
2. Curl and slide the tab through the two slits.

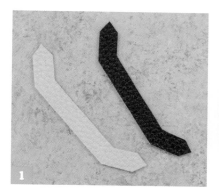

Simple
Leather Clutch

Carry the necessities for a night out on the town. This clutch will work well with genuine or faux leather or suede. I used a striped faux leather to make a striking statement!

SUPPLIES & MATERIALS

- Rotary or standard cutting blade
- 12" x 24" strong cutting mat
- 1 piece of faux leather, 10" x 17"
- Contrasting embroidery floss
- Needle
- 1 set of plastic snaps
- Snap pliers
- Simple Leather Clutch SVG file

BEFORE YOU BEGIN

- Supplies and instructions are for making one clutch.
- For more information on cutting faux leather, see page 22.
- Some cutting machines may struggle to cut the small holes in this project. If needed, use a leather punch to make the holes.

INSTRUCTIONS

1. Cut the faux leather piece.

2. Fold the leather in half and line up the holes on either side of the clutch. Hand-stitch each side with embroidery floss.

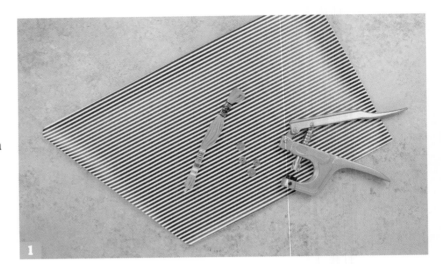

3. Insert the snaps through the holes and set them with the snap pliers. Make sure to position the snaps so they will snap correctly.

Geometric Paper Earrings

Perfectly match your accessories to your outfit with these trendy paper earrings. It is a great project for busting through paper scraps, and it's easy to reuse the jewelry findings in future projects. Try glitter cardstock for a lavish look!

SUPPLIES & MATERIALS

- Standard cutting blade
- 12" x 12" standard cutting mat
- 1 piece of yellow cardstock, 2" x 3"
- 1 piece of dark pink cardstock, 2" x 3"
- 1 piece of light pink cardstock, 2" x 3"
- 6 jump rings
- 2 fishhook earring findings
- Flat-nose pliers
- Geometric Paper Earrings SVG file

BEFORE YOU BEGIN

- Supplies and instructions are for making one pair of earrings.
- For more information on cutting cardstock, see page 18.

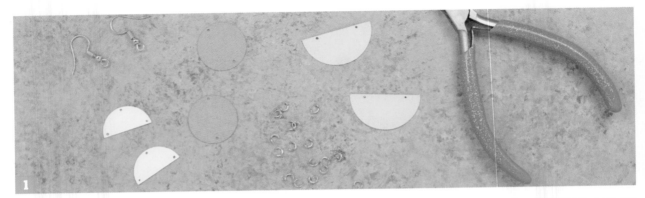

INSTRUCTIONS

1. Cut the cardstock pieces.

2. Open the jump rings and thread them through the holes in the earrings to connect the pieces. Clamp closed.

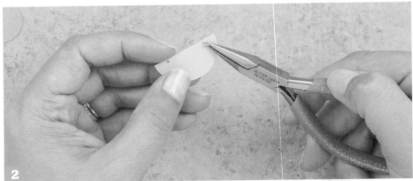

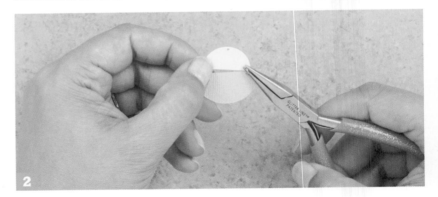

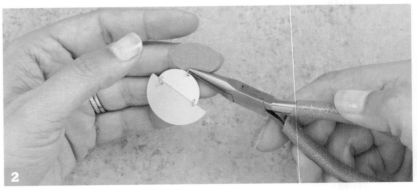

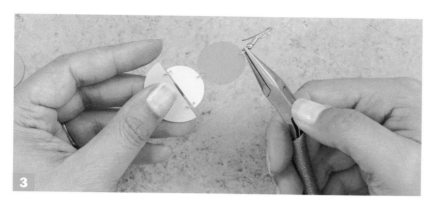

3. Add the fishhook earrings to the top holes to finish.

Rainbow Hoodie

Take a simple hoodie and make it your own using layered iron-on vinyl! Use these same techniques to make all sorts of apparel—vacation T-shirts, children's clothing, and more.

SUPPLIES & MATERIALS

- Standard cutting blade
- 12" x 12" standard cutting mat
- 1 piece of white iron-on vinyl, 2" x 7"
- 1 piece of pink iron-on vinyl, 3" x 4"
- 1 piece of yellow iron-on vinyl, 4" x 6"
- 1 piece of black iron-on vinyl, 3" x 3"
- Weeding tool
- Scissors
- Iron or Cricut EasyPress
- Pressing mat
- Pink hoodie
- Teflon sheet or pressing cloth
- Hoodie SVG file

BEFORE YOU BEGIN

- Supplies and instructions are for making one hoodie.
- For more information on cutting and layering iron-on vinyl, see page 18.
- To help keep the edges of the plastic carrier sheet from imprinting the iron-on vinyl I've already pressed, I've hand-trimmed close to the edge of the rainbow where it overlaps. It is a technique I often use, as it creates a cleaner project. You can also use the cut-through technique from page 19.
- For more information on heat settings, see page 19.

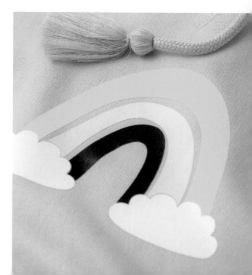

INSTRUCTIONS

1. Cut the iron-on vinyl pieces.

2. Weed out the negative material.

3. Place the pressing mat inside the hoodie.

4. Position the yellow piece and the clouds on the center of your hoodie to make sure you like the placement. Remove the yellow piece, leaving only the clouds.

5. Layer a Teflon sheet or pressing cloth on top of the clouds.

6. Following the manufacturer's instructions, use the iron or EasyPress to adhere the vinyl to the project.

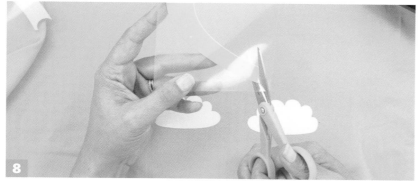

7. Peel off the plastic liner.

8. Trim around the bottom edges of the rainbow pieces with scissors.

9. Position the yellow layer of iron-on vinyl onto the project.

10. Layer a Teflon sheet or pressing cloth on top of the pieces.

11. Using the iron or EasyPress, apply firm pressure to your project.

12. Peel off the plastic liner.

13. Repeat with the other two layers.

14. Flip the hoodie over and press for 15 seconds from the back.

Tote Bag

This roomy tote is easy to make using your cutting machine's rotary blade. Choose a bright, colorful fabric for the shell and the lining and a contrasting solid fabric for the bottom. You could even personalize it with iron-on vinyl!

SUPPLIES & MATERIALS

- Rotary cutting blade
- 12" x 24" fabric or standard cutting mat
- 2 pieces of print fabric for the shell, 12" x 14"
- 2 pieces of print fabric for the lining, 12" x 18"
- 2 pieces of solid fabric for the shell bottom, 8" x 12"
- 2 pieces of fusible fleece, 12" x 18"
- Iron
- Pressing mat or ironing board
- Sewing machine and supplies
- 2 soft leather straps, 1" x 21"
- Embroidery floss
- Needle
- Tote Bag SVG file

BEFORE YOU BEGIN

- Supplies and instructions are for making one tote bag.
- For more information on cutting fabric, see page 22.
- I chose fusible fleece to line this tote, but you can use the interfacing of your choice.
- All seams are ¼".

INSTRUCTIONS

1. Cut the fabric and fusible fleece pieces.

2. Sew one shell and one shell bottom fabric piece together. Repeat.

3. Iron the fleece to the lining pieces of the bag.

4. With right sides together, sew the sides and bottom of the two shell pieces together.

5. Repeat with the fused lining pieces, leaving a 3" gap on the bottom for turning.

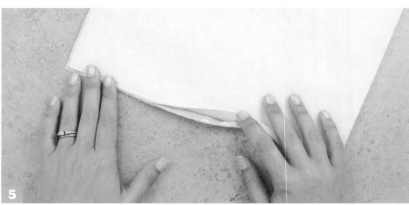

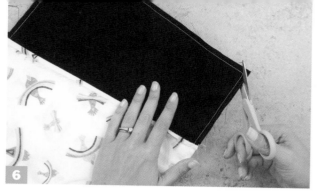

6. Clip the corners.

7. Turn the shell right side out and nestle it inside the lining, with right sides together and the side seams aligned. Sew both pieces together around the top opening.

8. Pull the shell through the gap left in the lining and close the gap with small hand stitches.

9. Topstitch the top of the tote bag.

10. Attach the handles by hand using the embroidery floss and burying the stitches within the layers of the bag so they do not show through the lining.

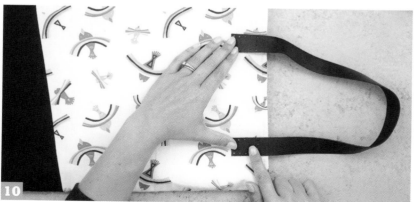

▲▲▲▲▲▲▲▲▲▲▲▲▲▲▲▲▲▲▲▲▲

Leather Tassel Key Chain

Adorn your tote bag, laptop case, and more with this stylish leather tassel! Your cutting machine cuts perfect fringe, so making this modern accessory is easy. This project works well with both genuine and faux leather or suede. You could even cut it out of felt!

SUPPLIES & MATERIALS

- ▪ Rotary or standard cutting blade
- ▪ 12" x 12" strong cutting mat
- ▪ 1 piece of black faux leather, 5" x 9"
- ▪ Hot glue gun
- ▪ 1 lobster claw key chain finding
- ▪ Leather Tassel Key Chain SVG file

BEFORE YOU BEGIN

- ▪ Supplies and instructions are for making one tassel.
- ▪ For more information on cutting faux leather, see page 22.

INSTRUCTIONS

1. Cut the faux leather pieces.

2. Fold the long, narrow piece in half and glue it to the top left side of the large tassel piece.

3. Apply a line of glue on the top edge and roll the leather into a tassel.

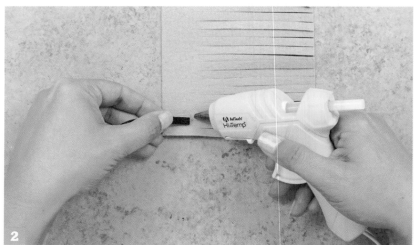

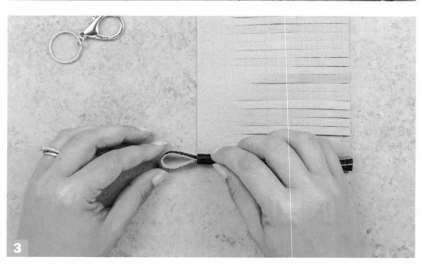

4. Glue the small leather piece around the top of the tassel to secure it.

5. Add the lobster clip to the loop to finish your tassel.

Party

Your cutting machine is your best friend when it comes to crafting for any party. From photo booth props to banners, cake toppers to favors—you can DIY pretty much everything you'll need for a fantastic fête!

MAGICAL
HAPPY

Rainbow Photo Booth Props

A party isn't complete without a set of fun photo booth props! Combine these with the paper fan backdrop for the perfect DIY photo booth. Use these SVG files to make shirts, tote bags, and other projects as well!

SUPPLIES & MATERIALS

- Standard cutting blade
- 12" x 12" standard cutting mat
- 2 sheets of white kraft board, 12" x 12"
- 1 sheet of pink cardstock, 12" x 12"
- 1 sheet of yellow cardstock, 12" x 12"
- 1 sheet of light blue cardstock, 12" x 12"
- 1 sheet of teal cardstock, 12" x 12"
- 1 sheet of navy blue cardstock, 12" x 12"
- 9 wooden dowels
- Spray paint (optional)
- Glue stick
- Hot glue gun
- Rainbow Photo Booth Props SVG file

BEFORE YOU BEGIN

- Supplies and instructions are for making nine photo booth props.
- For more information on cutting cardstock, see page 18.
- For more information on cutting kraft board, see page 18.
- To make the props sturdier, I cut the background layer from the white kraft board. You can also use standard white cardstock.

INSTRUCTIONS

1. If desired, spray-paint the wooden dowels in coordinating colors.

2. Cut the white kraft board pieces.

3. Cut the colored cardstock pieces.

4. Assemble the photo booth props using the glue stick.

5. Hot-glue a dowel to the back of each prop.

Confetti Table Runner

Transform a plain white table runner into a party table centerpiece! This confetti table runner is made using iron-on vinyl and decorated at each end with coordinating pom-pom trim.

SUPPLIES & MATERIALS

- Standard cutting blade
- 12" x 12" standard cutting mat
- White linen table runner, 6'
- 1 piece of pink iron-on vinyl, 12" x 12"
- 1 piece of yellow iron-on vinyl, 12" x 12"
- 1 piece of light blue iron-on vinyl, 12" x 12"
- 1 piece of teal iron-on vinyl, 12" x 12"
- 1 piece of navy blue iron-on vinyl, 12" x 12"
- Iron or Cricut EasyPress
- Pressing mat
- Teflon sheet or pressing cloth
- Pom-pom trim, about 1 yard
- Hot glue gun
- Confetti Table Runner SVG file

BEFORE YOU BEGIN

- Supplies and instructions are for making one 6' table runner.
- For more information on cutting iron-on vinyl with the cut-through technique, see page 19.
- For more information on heat settings, see page 19.

INSTRUCTIONS

1. Cut the iron-on vinyl pieces using the cut-through technique.

2. Place the table runner on the pressing mat. You will need to work in sections.

3. Randomly place the confetti pieces on the table runner.

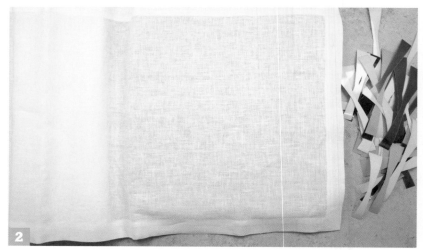

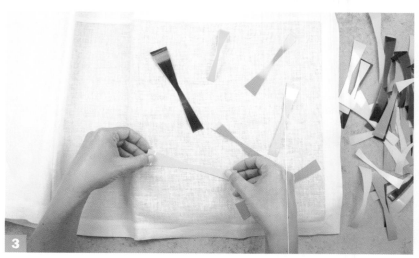

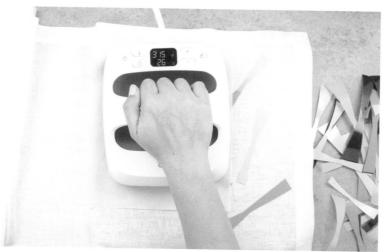

4. Layer a Teflon sheet or pressing cloth on top of the pieces.

5. Following the manufacturer's instructions, use the iron or EasyPress to adhere the vinyl to the project.

6. Peel off the plastic liner pieces.

7. Repeat with the rest of the pieces, working your way through the length of the runner.

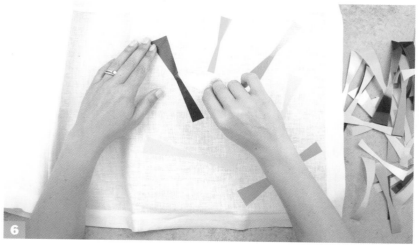

8. If you want to layer the confetti pieces, make sure to peel the liner off the bottom piece before pressing the second piece on top.

9. Sew or hot-glue a strip of pom-pom trim to each end of the table runner.

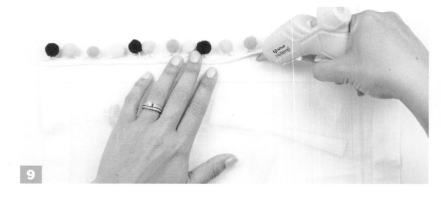

Felt Cake Stand Garland

Make any cake stand party-ready with this cute felt garland! Glue dots work well for attaching the garland to your cake stand. You can also cut this file in a larger size and use it to make a festive party backdrop.

SUPPLIES & MATERIALS

- Rotary or standard cutting blade
- 12" x 12" standard cutting mat
- 1 piece of pink felt, 2" x 9"
- 1 piece of yellow felt, 2" x 9"
- 1 piece of light blue felt, 2" x 9"
- 1 piece of teal felt, 2" x 9"
- 1 piece of navy blue felt, 2" x 9"
- 1 piece of white ribbon, 32"
- Hot glue gun
- Glue dots
- Felt Cake Stand Garland SVG file

BEFORE YOU BEGIN

- Supplies and instructions are for making a garland for an 8" cake stand. Add or remove felt pieces for larger or smaller cake stands.
- For more information on cutting felt, see page 20.

INSTRUCTIONS

1. Cut the felt pieces.
2. Adhere the pieces to the ribbon using hot glue, aligning the top of the piece to the top of the ribbon.
3. Attach to the cake stand edge using the glue dots.

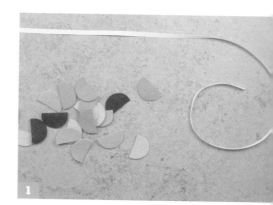

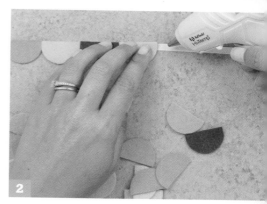

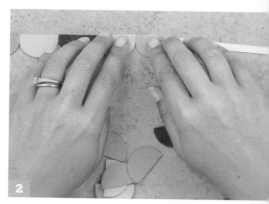

Rainbow Crowns

Forget traditional party hats and make these colorful rainbow crowns! They are simple to make with your electronic cutting machine using 12" x 24" cardstock sheets.

SUPPLIES & MATERIALS

- Standard cutting blade
- 12" x 24" standard cutting mat
- 1 sheet of pink cardstock, 12" x 24"
- 1 sheet of pink cardstock, 12" x 12"
- 1 sheet of teal cardstock, 12" x 24"
- 1 sheet of yellow cardstock, 12" x 12"
- 1 sheet of light blue cardstock, 12" x 12"
- 1 sheet of navy blue cardstock, 12" x 12"
- Glue stick
- Stapler
- Rainbow Crowns SVG file

BEFORE YOU BEGIN

- Supplies and instructions are for making four rainbow crowns.
- For more information on cutting cardstock, see page 18.

INSTRUCTIONS

1. Cut the cardstock pieces.
2. Assemble using the glue stick.
3. Wrap around the head to measure, then overlap the crown ends and staple to secure.

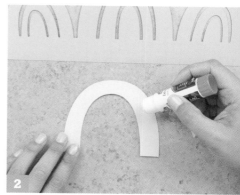

Fabric Tassels

Fabric tassels add a wonderful handmade dimension to any party theme, and they are easy to make using a cutting machine's rotary blade. They also look charming in nurseries and kids' rooms!

SUPPLIES & MATERIALS

- Rotary cutting blade
- 12" x 24" standard or fabric cutting mat
- 1 piece of fabric, 12" x 18", plus a small scrap
- Hot glue gun
- Ribbon
- Fabric Tassels SVG file

BEFORE YOU BEGIN

- Supplies and instructions are for making one tassel.
- For more information on cutting fabric, see page 22.
- I often use the uncut "extra" fabric around the cut project as my scrap for securing the tassel.

INSTRUCTIONS

1. Cut the fabric piece.

2. Starting at one uncut end, roll your fabric, untangling the fringe as you go.

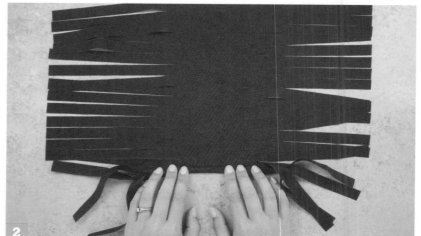

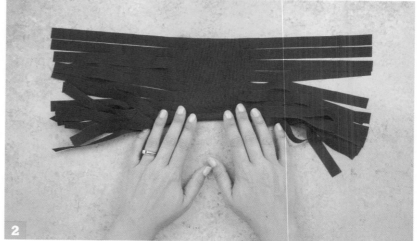

3. Bend in half to create a loop.

4. Use a scrap of fabric and hot glue to secure your tassel.

5. If you wish to make a tassel banner, repeat the steps with assorted fabrics and string them together with ribbon or twine.

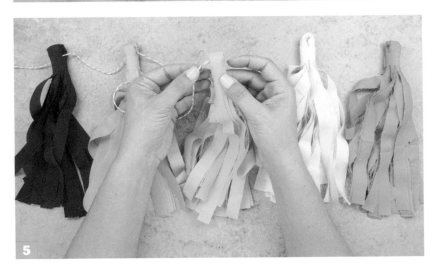

Popcorn Boxes

Make popcorn boxes and decorate them with adhesive vinyl! By using larger vinyl shapes, there's no need for transfer tape, as the vinyl alone is perfect for more delicate surfaces like paper.

SUPPLIES & MATERIALS

- Standard cutting blade
- 12" x 24" standard cutting mat
- 2 sheets of pink cardstock, 12" x 24"
- 2 sheets of teal cardstock, 12" x 24"
- 1 piece of pink adhesive vinyl, 5" x 6"
- 1 piece of teal adhesive vinyl, 5" x 6"
- Cutting machine scoring tool
- Hot glue gun
- Popcorn Boxes SVG file

Note. To change the score lines in the SVG file: (1) ungroup the project, (2) change the cut lines to score lines, and (3) attach the lines back to the project.

BEFORE YOU BEGIN

- Supplies and instructions are for making four popcorn boxes.
- For more information on cutting cardstock, see page 18.
- For more information on cutting adhesive vinyl, see page 20.

INSTRUCTIONS

1. Cut the cardstock and adhesive pieces.

2. Peel up the YUM pieces by hand and place them on one side of the popcorn box.

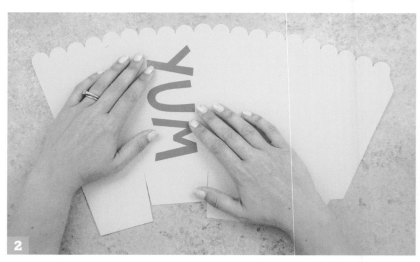

3. Fold along the score lines.

4. Assemble the popcorn box by hot-gluing the side flap and then the bottom flaps.

Happy Vibes Napkins

Iron-on vinyl is well suited for all sorts of paper and cardstock bases, like these napkins. Use this technique to personalize cardstock banners, notebook covers, greeting cards, and more!

SUPPLIES & MATERIALS

- Standard cutting blade
- 12" x 12" standard cutting mat
- 4 white paper napkins
- 1 piece of pink iron-on vinyl, 4" x 5"
- 1 piece of yellow iron-on vinyl, 4" x 5"
- 1 piece of teal iron-on vinyl, 4" x 5"
- 1 piece of navy blue iron-on vinyl, 4" x 5"
- Weeding tool
- Iron or Cricut EasyPress
- Pressing mat
- Teflon sheet or pressing cloth
- Happy Vibes Napkins SVG file

BEFORE YOU BEGIN

- Supplies and instructions are for making four napkins.
- For more information on cutting iron-on vinyl, see page 18.
- For more information on heat settings, see page 19.

INSTRUCTIONS

1. Cut the iron-on vinyl pieces.

2. Weed out the negative material.

3. Place a napkin on the pressing mat and position the image on the napkin.

4. Layer a Teflon sheet or pressing cloth on top of the project.

5. Following the manufacturer's instructions, use the iron or EasyPress to adhere the vinyl to the project.

6. Peel off the plastic liner.

7. Repeat with the other three napkins.

Rainbow Cake Topper

This bold cake topper looks great on top of cloudlike white frosting! Paint with your favorite craft paints or spray paint or leave it unfinished for a more rustic look.

SUPPLIES & MATERIALS

- Knife/kraft cutting blade
- 12" x 12" strong cutting mat
- 1 piece of basswood, 11" x 11"
- Acrylic craft paint (pink, yellow, light blue, teal, and navy)
- Paintbrush
- Hot glue gun
- Rainbow Cake Topper SVG file

BEFORE YOU BEGIN

- Supplies and instructions are for making one cake topper.
- For more information on cutting basswood, see page 21.

INSTRUCTIONS

1. Cut the basswood pieces.

2. Paint the basswood pieces using the craft paint.

3. Adhere the pieces together using hot glue.

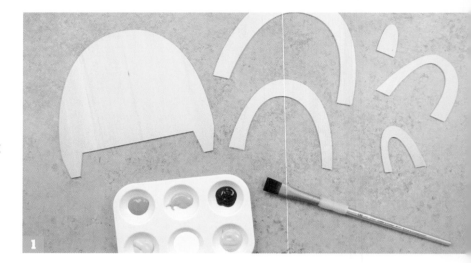

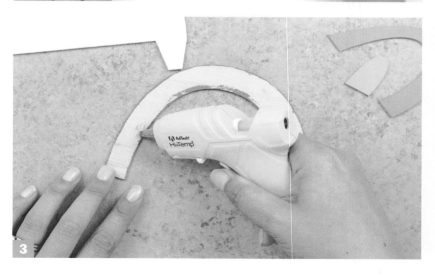

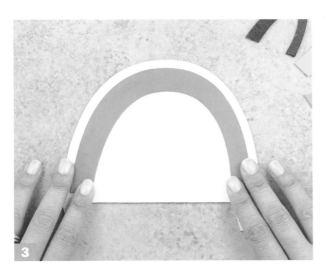

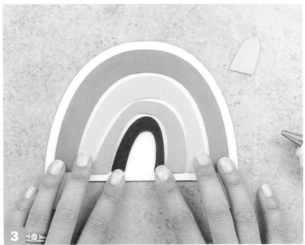

Paper Fan Garland

This paper fan garland works for virtually every type of party—choose scrapbook paper that coordinates with your party theme. I love making several garlands and layering them to create a stunning photography backdrop.

SUPPLIES & MATERIALS

- Standard cutting blade
- Knife/kraft cutting blade (optional)
- 12" x 12" standard and strong cutting mats
- 5 sheets of assorted scrapbook paper, 12" x 12"
- 1 sheet of chipboard, 11" x 11"
- Cutting machine scoring tool or scoring board
- Stapler
- Hot glue gun
- 6' of ⅝" ribbon
- Paper Fan Garland SVG file

Note. To change the score in the SVG file: (1) ungroup the project, (2) change the cut lines to score lines, and (3) attach the lines back to the project.

BEFORE YOU BEGIN

- Supplies and instructions are for making one 6' garland with five 11"-wide fans.
- Scrapbook paper works best—cardstock can be too heavy. For more information on cutting paper, see page 18.
- I've stabilized these paper fans using the chipboard. If your cutting machine does not have a knife/kraft blade to cut chipboard, you can cut the ¾" x 10" strips by hand with a ruler and a craft knife. For more information on cutting chipboard, see page 18.

INSTRUCTIONS

1. Score and cut the paper pieces using the standard cutting mat.

2. Cut the chipboard stabilizer strips using the strong cutting mat.

3. Accordion-fold the pieces along the score lines.

4. Fold the fan in half and staple its center.

5. Glue the two center edges together to create the fan shape.

6. Glue the top edges of the fan to the chipboard strips.

7. Repeat with the other four fans.

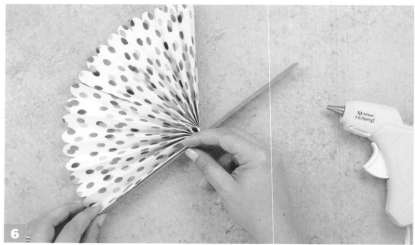

8. Glue all five fans to the ribbon to create the garland, leaving about 6" of ribbon on each end for hanging.

★★★★★★★★★★★★★★★

Baby

Design a beautiful nursery to lull the little one to sleep! The baby will be whisked off to dreamland with these sweet ideas made from iron-on vinyl, wood, felt, and more.

★★★★★★★★★★★★★★★★★★★★★★★

Star
Wall Art

Simple doesn't have to be boring! Use basswood to create this whimsical wall art and decorate the nursery with the twinkles from the night sky.

SUPPLIES & MATERIALS

- Knife/craft cutting blade
- 12" x 12" strong cutting mat
- 6 pieces of basswood, 11" x 11"
- Gray spray paint
- Yellow spray paint
- Teal spray paint
- Navy blue spray paint
- Adhesive strips
- Star Wall Art SVG file

BEFORE YOU BEGIN

- Supplies and instructions are for making 30 stars.
- For more information on cutting basswood, see page 21.

INSTRUCTIONS

1. Cut the basswood stars.

2. Spray-paint each piece.

3. Adhere them to the wall using the adhesive strips.

Constellation Blanket

Your little one will fall asleep under the stars with this dazzling constellation blanket. I've divided the SVG cut file into eight pieces, but when applied to the blanket, it looks like one large image. It is a big project, so take your time! The result is totally worth it.

SUPPLIES & MATERIALS

- Standard cutting blade
- 12" x 24" standard cutting mat
- Navy blue swaddle blanket
- 8 pieces of silver iron-on vinyl, 12" x 24"
- Weeding tool
- Iron or Cricut EasyPress
- Pressing mat or ironing board
- Teflon sheet or pressing cloth
- Constellation Blanket SVG file

BEFORE YOU BEGIN

- Supplies and instructions are for making one 46" x 46" blanket. The maximum size for this project is 46" x 46". If you want to make a larger blanket, you will need to use your cutting machine's design program to divide the SVG file further.
- For more information on cutting iron-on vinyl, see page 18.
- For more information on heat settings, see page 19. An ironing board is a good option for this project.
- The cut file is very forgiving—if you find your fabric has shifted under the EasyPress or it's not as big as you thought, you can easily trim the pieces down to fit.

INSTRUCTIONS

1. Cut the iron-on vinyl pieces.

2. Weed out the negative material.

3. Place the blanket on the pressing mat. Work in sections, starting on the lower left.

4. Position the first constellation piece on the blanket.

5. Layer a Teflon sheet or pressing cloth on top of the piece.

6. Following the manufacturer's instructions, use the iron or EasyPress to adhere the vinyl to the project.

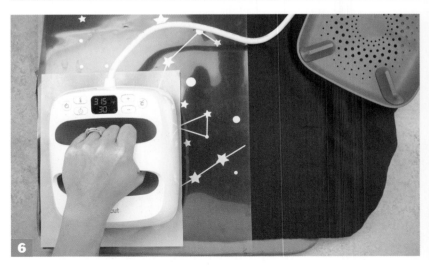

7. Peel off the plastic liner. If it does not peel easily, press for another 15 seconds.

8. Repeat for the rest of the pieces on the blanket, lining up the stars that connect each section.

9. Flip the blanket over and press each section for 15 seconds from the back.

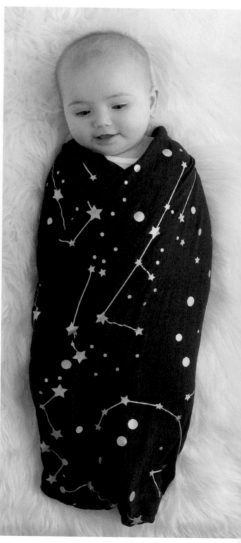

Mountain Pillow

★★★★★★★★★★★★★★★★★★★★★★★★

Bring the outdoors inside with this felt appliqué mountain pillow. It's a cozy addition to any room in your home, but I love it in the nursery.

SUPPLIES & MATERIALS

- ■ Rotary or standard cutting blade
- ■ 12" x 12" standard cutting mat
- ■ 2 pieces of navy blue fabric, 18" x 18"
- ■ 1 piece of white felt, 9" x 12"
- ■ 1 piece of gray felt, 9" x 12"
- ■ 1 piece of dark gray felt, 9" x 12"
- ■ Sewing machine and sewing supplies
- ■ Polyester fiberfill or 18" pillow insert
- ■ Mountain Pillow SVG file

BEFORE YOU BEGIN

- ■ Supplies and instructions are for making one 18" x 18" pillow.
- ■ For more information on cutting felt, see page 20.
- ■ All seams are ¼".
- ■ You can also hand-stitch the felt pieces to a purchased pillowcase or sew an envelope enclosure for the back and use a pillow form.

INSTRUCTIONS

1. Cut the felt pieces.

2. Pin the gray mountain pieces to one of the fabric squares as shown.

3. Machine-stitch the mountain pieces to the navy blue background.

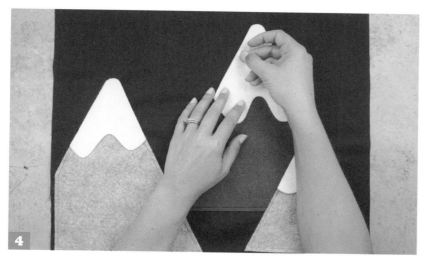

4. Pin the white snow pieces to the top of the gray mountain pieces.

5. Stitch the snow pieces in place.

6. With right sides together, pin the front and the back of the pillow.

7. Sew on all four sides, leaving a 3" gap on one side for turning.

8. Clip the corners, turn the pillow right side out, and press.

9. Fill the pillowcase with fiberfill.

10. Hand-stitch the gap closed.

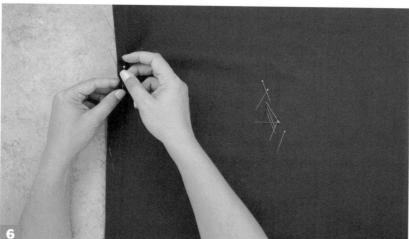

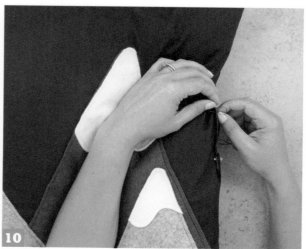

★★★★★★★★★★★★★★★★★★★★★★★★★★★

Dream Big Baby Onesie

Every baby deserves to dream big! This classic cutting machine project makes the perfect gift for a new arrival. I like using the small Cricut EasyPress for this project—it fits right between the seams, giving the perfect press.

SUPPLIES & MATERIALS

- Standard cutting blade
- 12" x 12" standard cutting mat
- White baby onesie
- 1 piece of teal iron-on vinyl, 2" x 5"
- 1 piece of navy blue iron-on vinyl, 4" x 5"
- Weeding tool
- Iron or Cricut EasyPress
- Pressing mat
- Teflon sheet or pressing cloth
- Dream Big Baby Onesie SVG file

BEFORE YOU BEGIN

- Supplies and instructions are for making one onesie.
- For more information on cutting iron-on vinyl, see page 18.
- For more information on heat settings, see page 19.

INSTRUCTIONS

1. Cut the iron-on vinyl pieces.

2. Weed out the negative material for each of the iron-on layers. Trim close to the edge of the letters so you can press both colors at the same time.

3. Place the onesie on the pressing mat and position the images.

4. Layer a Teflon sheet or pressing cloth on top of the pieces.

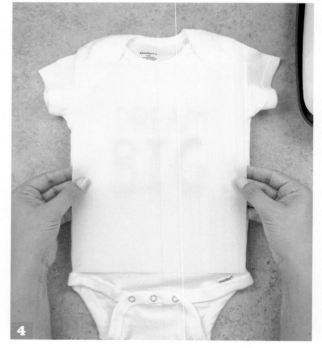

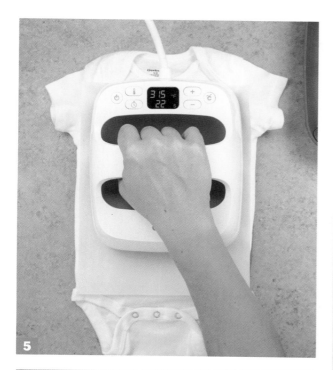

5

5. Following the manufacturer's instructions, use the iron or EasyPress to adhere the vinyl to the project.

6. Peel off the plastic liner.

7. Flip the onesie over and press for 15 seconds from the back.

6

Bandanna Bib

These bandanna-style bibs are the stylish answer to feeding time and keeping drool at bay! I've used cotton, but you can also cut them from flannel, muslin, fleece, or even minky. These bibs make a wonderful baby shower gift—personalize them by adding the new baby's name in iron-on vinyl!

SUPPLIES & MATERIALS

- Rotary cutting blade
- 12" x 24" fabric or standard cutting mat
- 1 piece of print fabric, 12" x 15"
- 1 piece of coordinating lining fabric, 12" x 15"
- Sewing machine and sewing supplies
- Iron
- 2 sets of plastic snaps
- Plastic snap pliers
- Bandanna Bib SVG file

BEFORE YOU BEGIN

- Supplies and instructions are for making one bib.
- For more information on cutting fabric, see page 22.
- All seams are ¼".

INSTRUCTIONS

1. Cut the fabric pieces.

2. With right sides together, layer the pieces and sew around the edge, leaving a 2" gap for turning.

3. Clip the rounded corners.

4. Turn the bandanna right side out.

5. Press the bandanna.

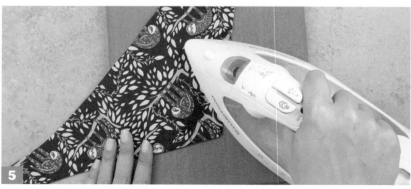

6. Topstitch around the bandanna, turning the gap edges in and closing it as you stitch.

7. Measure in ¾" from the corner end and set one plastic snap.

8. Measure in ¾" from that snap and set one more plastic snap.

9. Do the same on the other corner, positioning your snap pieces so they will snap correctly.

Hair Bow Clips

These adorable hair bows come together in just minutes! All you need is your cutting machine, faux leather, and a clip. Make a bunch for your bundle of joy!

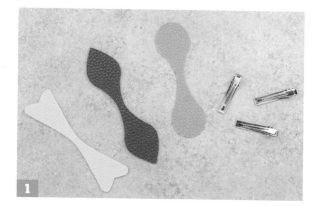

SUPPLIES & MATERIALS

- ◼ Rotary cutting blade or standard cutting blade
- ◼ 12" x 12" strong cutting mat
- ◼ 1 piece of yellow faux leather, 2" x 6"
- ◼ 1 piece of teal faux leather, 2" x 6"
- ◼ 1 piece of navy blue faux leather, 2" x 6"
- ◼ 3 crocodile hair clips, 1½"
- ◼ Hair Bow Clips SVG file

BEFORE YOU BEGIN

- ◼ Supplies and instructions are for making three clips.
- ◼ For more information on cutting faux leather, see page 22.

INSTRUCTIONS

1. Cut the faux leather pieces.
2. Tie each bow into a knot, leaving it a bit loose.
3. Insert the clip through the knot.
4. Tighten the bow.

Star Mobile

The floating moon and stars will soothe the baby while you make your way to the nursery! The interior ring of an embroidery hoop is the perfect size for the mobile.

SUPPLIES & MATERIALS

- Rotary or standard cutting blade
- 12" x 12" standard cutting mat
- 10" embroidery hoop
- 1 piece of white felt, 5" x 5"
- 2 pieces of light blue felt, 9" x 12"
- 2 pieces of teal felt, 9" x 12"
- 2 pieces of navy blue felt, 9" x 12"
- Sewing machine and sewing supplies
- Polyester fiberfill stuffing
- Embroidery floss
- 3 pieces of ribbon, 12" each
- Gold ring for hanging
- Star Mobile SVG file

BEFORE YOU BEGIN

- Supplies and instructions are for making one mobile.
- For more information on cutting felt, see page 20.
- I've machine-stitched the stars and moon, but you can hand-sew with a blanket stitch or whipstitch if you prefer.
- All seams are ¼".

INSTRUCTIONS

1. Cut the felt pieces.

2. Layer two felt stars together and stitch almost all the way around.

3. Insert a bit of stuffing.

4. Finish stitching around the star.

5. Repeat with the other stars and moon.

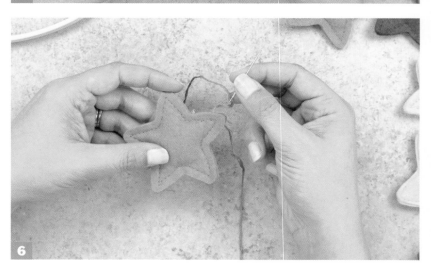

6

6. Hang the stars from the hoop with embroidery floss.

7. Hang the mobile by attaching three pieces of ribbon to the hoop and the gold ring.

8. Attach the moon to the ring so it hangs in the center.

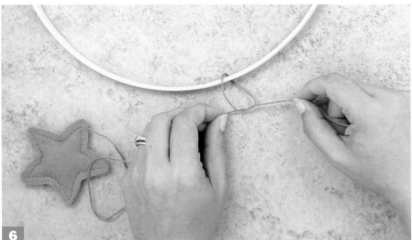

6

Cork Clock

This clock would be a great addition to any room in your home, but the "block" effect is particularly great for a nursery!

SUPPLIES & MATERIALS

- Rotary and knife/kraft cutting blade
- 1 piece of adhesive-backed cork, 12" x 12"
- 1 piece of chipboard, 12" x 12"
- Spray paint (light blue, teal, and navy blue)
- Ruler
- Pencil
- Painter's tape
- Drill and 5/16" drill bit
- Clock mechanism
- Cork Clock SVG file

BEFORE YOU BEGIN

- Supplies and instructions are for making one clock.
- For more information on cutting cork, see page 21.
- For more information on cutting chipboard, see page 18.
- To make the clock sturdy, I used the chipboard as a backing. You can also use several kraft board hexagons glued together. If you do this, have your cutting machine cut a 5/16" circle in the center of the hexagons so you don't need to drill a hole.

INSTRUCTIONS

1. Cut the cork and chipboard pieces.

2. Spray-paint each piece of cork with one of the three colors of spray paint.

3. Place a piece of painter's tape in the middle of the chipboard so it won't shred as you drill through it.

4. Draw lines from point to point to find the center of the hexagon.

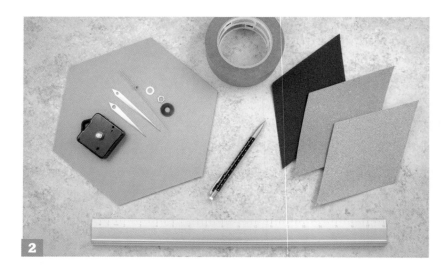

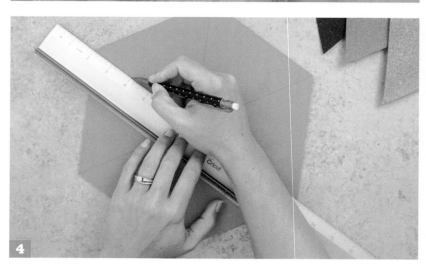

5. Drill a hole in the middle of the chipboard.

6. Remove the backing material and adhere the cork pieces to the chipboard.

7. Install the clock mechanism according to the manufacturer's instructions.

Acknowledgments

This book has been a labor of love, and I could not have done it
without the support of many people.

I'd like to thank my publishers for their guidance and support and the
wonderful manufacturers who have provided materials for the projects
in this book: Art Gallery Fabrics, Benzie Design, Color Shot, Cricut®,
Expressions Vinyl, and Xyron®.

I'd also like to thank my community of blogging friends for their creative
ideas and tireless troubleshooting. Blogging would be so lonely without you!
Special thanks to Heidi Kundin, Cheryl Spangenberg, Charynn Olsheski,
Angie Holden, and Amy Motroni for your unlimited support, humor, love, and
encouragement (as well as coffee and wine when desperately needed).

To my family, Judy Ashley, Bob Ashley, and Bonnie Lally, thank you for helping
me with the projects and photography for this book and keeping my boys
alive while I worked on it! My love goes out to all of you.

And finally, Ryan, Callum, and Sebastian, who sacrificed so much so I could
make this book happen. I could not ask for a more supportive family.
I love the three of you, *"a million a million."*

Index

Projects are indicated in *italics*.

BETTER DAY BOOKS®
HAPPY · CREATIVE · CURATED

Business is personal at Better Day Books. We were founded on the belief that all people are creative and that making things by hand is inherently good for us. It's important to us that you know how much we appreciate your support. The book you are holding in your hands was crafted with the artistic passion of the author and brought to life by a team of wildly enthusiastic creatives who believed it could inspire you. If it did, please drop us a line and let us know about it. Connect with us on Instagram, post a photo of your art, and let us know what other creative pursuits you are interested in learning about. It all matters to us. You're kind of a big deal.

it's a good day to have a better day!®

www.betterdaybooks.com

better_day_books